PASS IT ON

PASS IT ON

TRANSFERRING WEALTH,
WISDOM, AND FINANCIAL SMARTS
TO FUTURE GENERATIONS

———

LORI B. GERVAIS, CFP®,

ROGER G. GERVAIS, CFA®

LIONCREST

PUBLISHING

PASS IT ON

Transferring Wealth, Wisdom, and Financial
Smarts to Future Generations

ISBN   978-1-5445-0801-6 *Hardcover*
          978-1-5445-0800-9 *Paperback*
          978-1-5445-0799-6 *Ebook*

For our children: Anna, Will, and Jack

CONTENTS

INTRODUCTION

"Someone is sitting in the shade today because someone planted a tree a long time ago."

WARREN BUFFETT

You'd never guess it, if you sat down with the two of us in one of our offices. We'd greet you in professional suits, our degrees framed on the wall, a list of professional accolades discreetly displayed on certificates and plaques. We'd speak to you in calm, level voices, and we'd both look at you through our wire-framed glasses.

Most of our clients would never imagine we used to cruise the Midwest on a Harley Davidson motorcycle. In our early marriage, we loved adventuring together. We explored countries abroad, and then roared around the Great Lakes when we got home.

That is—until Anna was born.

Anna changed things. Rather than associating the Harley with a carefree cruise down the highway, we suddenly associated it with worst case scenarios. What if one of us died on that motorcycle?!

It didn't end there. The two of us are both financial advisors, and we'd spent most of our adult lives working to build our wealth. Pre-Anna, we'd thrown all our financial efforts into growing our retirement, or savings, or real estate investments. We cared about ourselves. Who else was there to care about?

Then, there *was* someone else to care about. Becoming parents felt like a gravitational shift; our perspective on everything expanded. We had to learn to be more selfless during late-night feedings, and diaper changes, and bleary-eyed mornings. We saw the world in new ways as we took our first walks with Anna, imagining things through her eyes. All of a sudden, everything our parents and grandparents taught us came to light. It was now our turn to provide purpose and a sense of financial security.

Our vision of wealth expanded too. We went from envisioning a future that only included the two of us, to a desire to allocate savings for our children—and *their* children. One of the first actions we took after Anna was born was opening a 529 college savings plan for her future education.

Then a fourth person joined us when Will was born—and then a fifth, with Jack. Now that Anna is old enough to observe our financial choices, there's even more to consider. We used to just set aside money for her. Now, we've realized, we actually need to teach her what to do with it!

Besides a financial education, there was still the Harley

factor. What if one of us died? What if both of us died? How would we make sure our children would be taken care of? How would we pass on our values? How could we perpetuate the wealth we have built? It was no longer enough to simply worry about ourselves. We had to start worrying about these precious lives we'd brought into the world as well.

WHY PASS IT ON

Kids change things. As parents with young children still in the home, we live out this fact every day. But as financial advisors, we know the considerations don't stop when the grown up kids move out. Many parents want to provide for their children over the course of their entire lives. Even after death, parents hope to pass on their wealth and values to their kids. They want to do everything possible to ensure their future generations enjoy security, fulfillment, and opportunity.

With our own children in mind, this book offers observations and tips that we've gleaned from our experience as financial advisors. It aims to help families effectively pass on their wealth, values, and financial literacy to future generations. We don't want to "pass it on" merely to perpetuate wealth—and from our experience as financial advisors, we know that's the case for most families. For most of us, passing it on aims to accomplish much more than that:

1. It's about providing financial security to our children in the event of an untimely passing.
2. It's about reducing financial constraints, so our children can pursue their passions and avail themselves of opportunities to grow.

3. It's about teaching our children the rewards of making a perpetual impact on family and community.
4. It's about promoting and facilitating creativity and entrepreneurship.
5. It's about teaching our children and grandchildren to recognize their good fortune, so that they're inspired to live with gratitude and generosity.
6. It's about learning to take a long view with the time horizons on our financial goals, ensuring that our strategy (and emotions) can weather short-term market volatility and set future generations up for success.
7. It's about educating our kids in financial literacy, ensuring they know how to avoid destructive financial habits and practice healthy ones.

In short, for us and countless other families, passing it on means setting our kids and grandkids up for success—not just financially, but in terms of their values, habits, and available opportunities.

PASSING ON WEALTH: SUCCESS OR SELF-SABOTAGE?

We work with families in nearly every stage of life, from elderly grandparents who want to solidify their estate plans, to young adults who are just beginning to think of establishing financial security for their young children. Often, we work across that span of generations within the same family.

There's never any shortage of good intentions; parents nearly always want to care for their children and subsequent generations in a loving way that blesses them financially. Often, those good intentions are paired with wise financial stewardship—when the older generations thoughtfully, deliberately, and intentionally help their younger generations learn about money and take up the Family Vision for wealth. However, sometimes the good intentions can lead to pitfalls in passing on wealth. These pitfalls can easily set heirs up for failure rather than success.

Sometimes, we see parents with kids still at home focus both on financial security *and* financial education. They set up college funds and life insurance, while also educating their kids financially. They give their children practice in investments and money management. They teach their kids that the money is not principally for their own enjoyment—it's also to share, and give, and pass on to future generations.

But we also see other parents who, despite their best efforts to do everything right, are not having discussions with their kids about how to handle finances wisely in the future. The focus is simply on providing for them. In the midst of all the soccer games and ballet lessons *educating* them in financial literacy is a lost priority. These families have helped us realize that financial literacy is something you have to intentionally build into your children's experience.

We've learned from parents further down the line, as well. Many of these parents funded their children's activities when they were young, and they now feel the natural desire to continue sharing their good fortune as the kids become adults. We can see how emotionally rewarding it is for our clients to gift potentially large sums of money on a regular basis to their adult children during the college years, into marriage, and throughout their adult lives. (Often, these gifts can be a smart financial strategy as well, helping to reduce future estate taxes.)

Sometimes, these financial gifts lead to all good things. We see parents with adult children intentionally communicate with their kids about financial gifts and expectations. These families know it's *okay* to talk about money. They don't hide their financial dealings from their children—they discuss it at an age-appropriate level. Rather than being ashamed of their wealth, or flaunting it with enormous purchases that drain their net worth, they *use* it. They save, they spend, they invest, and they give. For the most part, we see these children turn into prosperous, successful adults who live meaningful lives.

But sometimes, we see these financial gifts go awry. Any number of variables can turn these well-intended gifts from wealthy parents into a stumbling block for their adult children—a lack of open dialogue, financial literacy, or even a persuasive spouse can lead the recipients of those gifts to spending choices that the parents wouldn't agree with. Unbeknownst to the parents, those gifts could be funding a drug or gambling habit, encouraging living beyond their means, spendthrift behavior, and so on. These are real risks that warrant scrutiny. Often, the adult children can come to depend on financial gifts from their parents. Instead of developing maturity as a financial steward of the family wealth, they develop enabling behavior.

We also see benefactors at the end of their lives, doing their best to sort out how much to give, and to whom, and to what, and when. Sometimes, this is a gratifying experience, as parents affirm the wisdom and responsibility they've seen in their children. But other times, we see these elderly parents rearrange their estate plans, as they anxiously express concern that their children haven't developed disciplined financial habits. They want to continue providing for their family but recognize that their children aren't prepared to wisely steward the financial assets. So, in their children's best interests, they add constraints to their estate.

Even after the patriarchs or matriarchs pass away, the pitfalls can continue. We have seen grown heirs harbor anger toward their well-meaning parents for all the legal control mechanisms of their estates. The heirs usually don't think they've done anything wrong and feel their parents' restrictions are malicious. Sometimes they even come to assume the parents didn't love them. The parents may have set up their estate constraints as a way to lovingly provide for their children over their lifetimes, but the children may easily misinterpret those constraints as *unloving*.

A family may have years' worth of great memories boating together at the cabin, but a badly planned inheritance can wreak havoc on that camaraderie. Siblings fight over Dad's autographed baseball, or Mom's wedding ring, or who got how much. We hate seeing families fall apart like that, and we know it's even worse for the families themselves.

It's never the parents' intention to set their children up for failure. Nearly all the people we work with intend to be helpful and supportive to their heirs. Despite those good intentions though, it can go the wrong way. We see it all the time. However, we have also seen parents successfully navigate these risks by coaching the kids on money, staying engaged with them, providing accountability or connecting them with a wealth advisor.

This book is for anyone who wants to learn how these successful families do it. It's for parents and grandparents who want to be intentional about cultivating financially savvy kids—kids who go on to handle wealth well and use it to contribute to society, not just consume. It's also for people who want to be aware of the potential dangers in passing on wealth—people who want to increase their own financial literacy and pass that knowledge on to future generations.

OUR STORIES

We'd like you to be able to trust our recommendations and have a sense of where we're coming from. People's advice is usually motivated by what they value—so, we'd like to help you understand the values that act as the foundation for our suggestions.

Like everyone, the two of us have our own "financial backstories." We each came into our marriage with ideas about money that were heavily influenced by our education and upbringing. Here's a bit of the story, from each of us.

LORI'S STORY

I grew up in central Maine, and I don't remember worrying about money as a child. There always seemed to be enough available for gifts at Christmas, or a new car when we needed one. Even though we didn't often talk about money, I managed to internalize certain disciplines just by watching my parents' example. I watched them successfully navigate union strikes and career changes while still providing financial stability for our family. In retrospect, I realize my parents must have worked hard, sacrificed, and saved to achieve their financial security, and they passed those values on to me.

They also helped me make smart decisions about discretionary spending. When I whined about wanting a TV or a phone in my room—"Because all the other kids have them!"—they never gave in to my protests. They took care of my needs, and those weren't needs. I was expected to take care of "the wants." Starting around age twelve, I started finding ways to make spending money. I started off strawberry picking, then babysitting, and eventually I was a waitress.

My parents always made a point to pay off their credit card every month, and turned those bill payments into teachable moments for us kids. I always assumed that I needed to have sufficient cash to cover whatever I wanted to buy, which meant I learned to live within my means. Regular tithing and church attendance ingrained the expectation that part of my earnings were intended to go toward charity. I also saw my parents volunteer constantly in our church and community, which expanded the idea of giving as part of a lifestyle.

As the youngest in my family, I took a lot of cues from my older siblings, and that included spending habits. I'd watched my older brother save up for his first car, so I expected that I would have to save up for mine too. I was intent on going to college, but assumed I would have to work my way through and take out loans. It was a pleasant surprise when my parents told me they would help cover the cost! In general, it was always my expectation that if I wanted to retire early or buy a house, I was responsible for making that happen.

When I was one of the only kids in my high-school class to actually enjoy the accounting and tax preparation classes, I figured I had found my calling. But I wanted to do more than count money; I wanted to *organize* money. Plus, I wanted to work with people as a major part of my job. I got a picture of how I might do that when an inspirational woman came to a school career fair. She was a stockbroker, and gave me my first glimpse of a woman in a high-powered financial advising role.

I shifted my direction toward the wider-ranging area of finance. I pursued a number of roles within the field, always looking to get at the *why* beneath investment strategies. I liked thinking of the family components—college, generational wealth, estate planning, and organizing a much bigger picture. I was fascinated with how the building blocks could all come together to build a structure, each structure's construction unique to the needs of each family.

Eventually, the building blocks came together in a very particular structure for me—a brick structure, to be exact. One fateful day, I knocked on the door of Baird with my paper résumé in hand. I started at an entry-level position, and quickly worked my way up as a financial advisor and CERTIFIED FINANCIAL PLANNER™ professional.

I'm thankful to have achieved success in my career and to have been recognized nationally for my contributions as a financial advisor. The accolades are affirming, but what remains most meaningful to me is evidence that I'm helping people. I was inspired to pursue financial advising by a woman stockbroker, and was mentored along the way by another smart woman, Barbara Sweeney, eventually becoming her business partner. In the spirit of their mentorship, I devote a lot of time toward helping women achieve greater financial empowerment. I mentor women as clients and also in several volunteer groups.

As an adult, I can look back and see the values that my parents passed on to me: hard work, giving, generosity, delayed gratification, and financial pragmatism. Those are the same values that guide me professionally, and which Roger and I hope to pass on to Anna, Will, and Jack.

ROGER'S STORY

I grew up in a rural part of Maine. I was surrounded by uncles, aunts, cousins, and other extended family, most of who lived along my same road. It was a farm community, and we didn't think of money as our source of security. We relied on the land and on each other. I never attached my worth, or anyone's worth, to money. I'm thankful for that.

My aunt grew an enormous garden and shared the vegetables with nearly everyone we knew. When my parents built their house, we had relatives over on one weekend to put up the walls, and they came back to put up the roof on another weekend. When winter came, I remember conversations about who needed more firewood, or help fixing their storm windows—and then the community would come together to help. Generosity and giving were a way of life.

My family struggled financially, growing up—a lot. My parents filed for bankruptcy around the same time they filed for divorce. That must have been a crazy period for them, because my younger brother was born around the same time. Although I had never thought much of money before then, suddenly, at age ten, financial stress became a fact of life. I have memories of waking up in the middle of the night and seeing my mother at the kitchen counter. She had her checkbook in hand, and bills would be spread all across the counter. She was tireless in her efforts to keep us afloat.

In a rural community, it's a lot easier to start working young—so I got to work. My mom found me some lawn mowing jobs when I was about ten, and once I got a little older, I started cutting wood and hauling hay. By the time I was fifteen, I had picked more vegetables and berries than I could name. Although I'm sure my family could have used my income, my mom never asked for it. My money was my money—but my mom made sure I knew how to manage it. She set me up with a bank account and made me balance my checkbook.

I have a distinct memory from high school when all the previous assumptions I'd had about money were upended. One of my teachers gave me a worksheet which depicted a graph showing the exponential growth of compound interest. The worksheet showed that if we invested a certain amount of money every year while we were still young, we would end up being millionaires by the time we were in our sixties. That concept floored me. Here was a formula to achieve wealth simply by starting smart and starting early. Given the financial stress I'd watched my family endure throughout my adolescence, this was a big deal.

As I neared graduation, someone passed on the wisdom that if I had good grades and went to the University of Maine for engineering, I could apply for a full-tuition scholarship. After growing up doing carpentry with my grandfather, engineering appealed to me. I loved math, and definitely loved the prospect of earning a good income. I applied for the scholarship and got it.

I liked engineering. It resonated with the lifestyle I'd grown up with in my rural community, which required us to problem solve using the materials at hand. I worked as an electrical engineer and engineering manager at Rockwell Automation in Milwaukee for the first decade of my career, constantly using numbers to figure out solutions for our clients. Still, the world of finance remained intriguing to me. Being married to Lori, I was able to view a financial career from a front row seat. The math, the problem solving, the satisfaction of finding a good solution—it all seemed similar to the work I did as an engineer, but seemed to have a more immediate impact on families. I liked that, and I began to pursue Master's-level coursework in finance.

I had already achieved a graduate degree in finance when Lori's partner announced her retirement. Lori and I had often discussed how her high net worth clients really would be best served by a team, and I was ready to make a career change. To build the deepest level of investment knowledge, I went on to become a holder of the right to use the Chartered Financial Analyst® designation. I poured myself into the intricacies of investments, while Lori was able to pursue even deeper expertise on financial planning.

Like Lori, I've enjoyed finding ways to give back to our

community. I have served on the finance team at our church and have fun coaching the kids' sports teams. I like working with Lori in our respective roles as we team up to help our clients, and continue to enjoy the element of problem solving in my profession. As a dad, I'm trying to help our kids develop the same appreciation for hard work, community, and family that was shown to me.

Lori and I have talked often about the values we hope to pass on to our kids one day, some of the same values that the two of us were taught by our own parents. However, we didn't consider that there would be any urgency to those life lessons until a tragedy hit our community.

A SOBERING REALIZATION

Not long ago, a person we cared about greatly was diagnosed with an aggressive form of cancer. This person was a major influencer in our lives and around our same age. His children are the same ages as our children. Our community rallied around his family and had high hopes for his healing. Unfortunately, it was only a matter of months from our friend's diagnosis to his passing.

The two of us were shaken by his death. We realized that either one of us—or even both of us—could go at any time. We began to think about all that we still wanted to tell our kids, and felt new urgency to make sure they would be taken care of. Given the business we're in, we had already set up our guardians and overall estate planning—but there was more we wanted to do for them. We wanted to make sure our kids would have a way to understand our values and become financially literate.

Suddenly, this book came to the forefront of our conversations.

The two of us could think of all sorts of lessons that we still wanted to share with our three children. What if we were denied that opportunity? Whether they were learning lessons about money, or life, or morality—our kids would gather influence from *someone*. We wanted them to get those lessons from us.

Some parents are experts in medicine, or construction, or education. Our expertise is in finance. That's the subject where we most want to pass on knowledge to our kids. However, at age three, Jack isn't ready to comprehend a concept like compound interest—so we decided we'd better get it all on paper.

WHAT TO EXPECT

We work with people in all stages of life, and we've written this book to accommodate that span of generations. For each topic, we address how concepts can impact people at different stages of life, looking at children, young people, middle-aged adults, and elderly benefactors.

We'll cover:

- How to build a Family Vision for your wealth that will help it last for generations and provide your family with a values-based, core identity,
- Ways to influence and communicate with your kids about financial habits so they develop sound money management practices,

- Ways you can educate and provide financial experiences to your kids to promote their financial literacy,
- Practical considerations for legacy and estate-planning, including legal tools, and
- The potential dangers in handling finances, particularly when dealing with large estates.

Here's what this book is *not*: this is not a textbook, crammed with facts and statistics. It's not a series of promises. We know our advice is not the only way to be successful. We'll give you our advice and recommendations, but what you do with those is up to you.

It's also not a book for people who live by the philosophy of "dying with one penny." There are people out there who believe in spending all their money while they're still alive, and that's a legitimate value. But—admittedly—that's not our value. This book is for people who want to pass *on* their wealth to future generations.

In other words, this book is for us. This book is for our kids. This book is for our clients. It's an opportunity for us to pass on the financial wisdom we've learned along the way, so that the people we care about can pass it on, too.

PART ONE

VISION AND VALUES

Codify a Family Vision around your wealth and develop values related to family stewardship. Help your children internalize those values by modeling good financial habits, sharing stories of family history, and surrounding them with good influences.

CHAPTER ONE

————

VISION, VALUES, AND THE POWER OF OBLIGATION

"If you are working on something that you really care about, you don't have to be pushed. The vision pulls you."

STEVE JOBS

We recently stumbled upon a "diamond in the rough" real estate opportunity when a house in our neighborhood was put up for sale. Over a series of discussions, the two of us considered that the house might be a good investment for our family. We could fix it up and improve the overall condition of our street; we could bring in renters and earn some rental income. So, we decided to move forward on the purchase.

Now, *we* had put considerable thought into purchasing this rental home, but we *didn't* put much thought into communicating the purpose for the rental to our kids. That became abundantly clear when Lori picked up Anna from a playdate at one of our neighbors' houses. Anna, wanting to be friendly, told her buddy, "Next time, we can play in my new playhouse!"

Yikes! Anna had gotten the idea that our new investment property was one giant toy for her and her friends to play in! Mortified, Lori quickly tried to explain to the other mom what the actual status of the rental house was. Then, at dinner that night, we corrected our mistake and made a point to have a crystal-clear conversation with our kids about the *purpose* of this major new purchase.

"It's not a playhouse, even though we've been letting you play in the yard," we clarified. "We're going to fix up this house and then rent it to some new neighbors. We're going to help our neighborhood look a little nicer, and earn some money for big things down the road, like your college education and our retirement."

Our seven-year-old quickly got on board. He piped up: "Can *I* make some money with the rental?" The two of us laughed. That conversation continues to be ongoing!

The experience made one point abundantly clear: **kids will develop a vision for family wealth, whether or not you're intentional about communicating the vision you want them to have.** We never intended to communicate to Anna that this rental was her personal playhouse—but after a few play sessions in the back yard, she made that inference on her own. Similarly, if we take our kids on trips to theme parks or Yellowstone, but never bother communicating that our hard work has allowed us to fund these experiences, they might develop a misconception of where money comes from.

Jump ahead twenty years, and the vision that kids had for wealth when they were young—which may have seemed harmless at the time—can now turn into major roadblocks to their maturity and success. If we let Anna continue under the impression that the rental was her personal playhouse, she would probably have unrealistic expectations about her standard of living as an adult!

We want our kids to have a healthy understanding of the purpose of money, and we know most parents feel the same way, regardless of how old their children are. In fact, ensuring that adult children share your vision for passing on wealth becomes increasingly important the older they get. In our experience, that most critical test of your kids' financial values occurs in the final steps of estate planning. When your children inherit your wealth, will they perpetuate the wealth or will they buy themselves big toys? Kids that inherit money should understand and acknowledge that they may be lucky— that they may be starting the game of life two steps ahead. If they appreciate and respect how they got there, then they in turn will more likely be better stewards of their money.

You don't need to wonder. Families can set their children up for success by having intentional conversations about their family's vision for wealth.

FORMING A FAMILY VISION

Forming a Family Vision gives your family a game plan. It helps everyone get on the same page and crystallizes your family's core values. We believe having a plan like this in place is crucial for a successful transfer of wealth—and values—down the road.

One summer, I had the crazy idea to sign up for six triathlons. I had never done a single triathlon before; I don't
know why I thought this was a good idea. I think it was
born out of an exuberant post-work-out high after a Spin-
ning class when I was talking with some friends from the
gym. Regardless, I had signed up for six triathlons, and I
was committed.

Also, I barely knew how to swim.

To get myself from A to Z, I needed a game plan. I started
by seeking out a coach to help me learn the right type
of swim stroke and breathing mechanisms—because, as I
was informed, it's not a good idea to try to doggy-paddle
a mile-long swim. But it wasn't just physical preparation
that was required; I also had to mentally prepare. When
the gun goes off, and everyone runs from the beach into
the water—and when you get kicked in the face (because
you do)—those are anxiety-inducing experiences! I had to
mentally prepare for those challenges so I wouldn't quit
or fall far behind.

I had a strict training schedule and a nutritional regimen. I
even practiced the transfers—changing out of my wetsuit
to get onto my bike, and then shifting from my bike into
the run. I had to have a plan.

The plan derived from a clear goal, and it required physical, mental, and emotional preparation. I needed a coach
and a schedule. I also had to stay disciplined. In the end,
it all paid off. My first triathlon was a short "Sprint," but
by the end of the summer, I had completed what they

call an Olympic-length triathlon. I'd also improved as a swimmer!

In the same way, achieving a goal like passing on your wealth, values, and financial knowledge to your kids requires a *game plan*. Building and retaining your family wealth takes preparation, thoughtfulness, and communication. You need to create shared ownership of your family's goals, and you all need to buy into the same strategies. How do you do this? You come up with a Family Vision. **A Family Vision essentially answers the question, "What is money for?"** Or, put another way, "What is the purpose of our money?"

This seems like an obvious question, but there's often not an obvious answer. Think of a newlywed couple who—unknowingly—come into their marriage with two totally different visions of how to deal with money. The wife expects to have nice things: flashy cars, designer clothes, and a plush home. She expects that they will earn a lot, and spend a lot. The husband is more of a Scrooge McDuck—he's focused on accumulation. He's not interested in financing a Mercedes Benz; he'd much prefer to live in a studio apartment and save as much as possible. Until these two arrive at a shared Family Vision for their wealth, there will be conflict, frustration, and a sense that each spouse is undermining the other spouse's goals.

It's counter-productive at best when family members have different visions for the family wealth, especially across generations. At worst, it can destroy a family's estate—and even the family itself. The authors of *Preparing Heirs: Five Steps to a Successful Transition of Family Wealth and Values* note that the primary reason for an unsuccessful transition of wealth is due to the "breakdown of trust and communication within the family."[1] In other words, if a family wants to perpetuate wealth *they've got to get on the same page.* There needs to be trust, and shared ownership of the vision.

Corporate America gets this. Most large, thriving companies have a clearly defined mission statement. They have guiding principles, quarterly goals, and five-year plans. They have documents describing their company culture. Collectively, these documents and goals help everyone work toward a common goal. An article published by *The New York Times* pointed out how valuable this same process can be for families:

> "Jim Collins, a management expert and author of *Good to Great*, [said] that successful human enterprises of any kind, from companies to countries, go out of their way to capture their core identity. In Mr. Collins's terms, they 'preserve core, while stimulating progress.' The same applies to families, he said. Mr. Collins recommended that families create a mission statement similar to the ones companies and other organizations use to identify their core values."[2]

When everyone shares the same vision, momentum and efficiency can increase. The same is true for managing wealth within a family.

1 Williams, Roy O., and Vic Preisser. *Preparing Heirs: Five Steps to a Successful Transition of Family Wealth and Values.* Bandon: Robert D. Reed Publishers, 2015.

2 Feiler, Bruce. "The Stories That Bind Us." The New York Times. March 15, 2013. Accessed May 22, 2019. https://www.nytimes.com/2013/03/17/fashion/the-family-stories-that-bind-us-this-life.html.

We've been talking about a financial Family Vision, but some families want to take it a step further, and outline a comprehensive mission statement for their family. Research shows that when families rally around a common vision, their bond is strengthened across generations and children show more resilience through adolescence. One study makes the point:

> "Other data indicated that… regular family dinners, yearly vacations, and holiday celebrations occur more frequently in families that have high levels of cohesiveness and that they contribute to the development of a strong sense of what we have called the **intergenerational self**. It is this intergenerational self and the personal strength and moral guidance that seem to derive from it that are associated with increased resilience, better adjustment, and improved chances of good clinical and educational outcomes."[3]

Do you want to pass on your wealth and values to future generations? As an added bonus, would you like your kids to have more grit, have better mental health, perform better in school, and show greater ease in adjusting to unfamiliar contexts? Creating a Family Vision helps lead to all of these benefits. When families take steps to cultivate a family identity, they give their children a strong sense of self and history, which gives them more inner strength. When children are aware of their family's history and values, they're more likely to feel a positive obligation toward future generations.

---

3   Duke, Marshall P., Amber Lazarus, and Robyn Fivush. "Knowledge of Family History as a Clinically Useful Index of Psychological Well-being and Prognosis: A Brief Report." *Psychotherapy: Theory, Research, Practice, Training* 45, no. 2 (2008): 268-72. Accessed May 22, 2019. doi:10.1037/0033-3204.45.2.268.

HOW DO YOU DRAFT A FAMILY VISION?

You can write your Family Vision down—or not. It can be formal, or informal. You can hold a family meeting and have a boisterous brainstorming session, or quietly trade notes after doing some journaling on your own. Some families find it helpful to have a third party, like their financial advisor, initiate the conversation. How you choose to start talking about a Family Vision is up to you. What's important is that the conversation *starts*.

The wealth management publication *Worth* affirms that forming a Family Vision helps strengthen family bonds, sets up a sense of responsibility in younger generations, and helps pass on family values. This can be especially valuable, they note, for high net worth families. They recommend considering the following points in your conversations about a Family Vision:[4]

1. Core principles and tenets that define the family.
2. Traditions the family wants to preserve.
3. The impact the family wants to have on society.
4. How the family's vision and values should govern the deployment of resources.
5. The responsibilities of each family member to uphold the core values.

So how do you collect all that information? Families can start the process by coming up with some key stories that feel connected to a family's financial journey and core val-

---

4   Nagarajan, Kamesh. "How Can You Pass down Your Values to Your Children?" Worth, March 26, 2019. https://www.worth.com/advice/how-can-you-pass-down-your-values-to-your-children/.

ues.[5] Maybe you recall how Grandma would sew dresses through the night to put your mom through private school. Maybe it's remembering the long, hard, horrible year when Dad was out of work. Even better, if your family has a property for you to connect with where it all began, visit that place. It will remind you and your children of your family history and the legacy of sacrifice, which will influence the shape of your own Family Vision.

If you can, go back three generations in considering these memories. It's these deeply buried memories from your family history that will most consistently inform your attitudes about money—and it's important for the Family Vision to reflect your authentic core beliefs, otherwise, it won't have any sticking power. Then, note some of the themes that arise in those stories. What values seem to come up repeatedly? What are some of the guiding principles that your family has lived by? What challenges had to be overcome, and how?

Use those stories as a jumping off point for discussing your own financial values and experiences. Consider what values you want to perpetuate in your family, and what values you might want to change, or revise. Think about what you want *your* family's guiding principles to be, as you handle wealth. Once you've determined these guiding principles and values, think about your family's answer to the question, "What is money for?"

Together as a family, come up with a Family Vision state-

5   The Vanguard Group. "Drafting Your Family Mission Statement." PDF. Valley Forge, PA: Vanguard, 2017. https://advisors.vanguard.com/iwe/pdf/FASGPCMS. pdf. (May 17, 2019)

ment which incorporates those key values, priorities, and guiding principles. Some families create a document which each family member signs and dates, providing clear evidence of everyone's buy-in. That may seem overly formal to some; to others, it might seem reassuring. This process will look different for everyone.

The Lottery Litmus Test and Monopoly Measure

If your children are young, there's a good chance they may not know how to engage in a conversation about "financial priorities" yet — but, with a little creativity, you can still get them to answer the question, "What is money for?" Try asking each family member, "If you won the lottery today, what would you do with the money?"

"I'd buy a mansion!"

"I'd put it into my savings account and let it get even bigger."

"I'd take all my friends to Disneyland!"

Each person's answer will serve as a litmus test, revealing their financial values. In fact, this would be a useful question for anyone looking to get an idea about how another person views money — someone you're dating, for instance. The answers to this question will give you a sense of the other person's financial values, and provide a starting point for conversation. Within a family, you can talk to your kids about the potential outcome of each of those "lottery-winning decisions" and help them better understand the values you hope to cultivate in your own family.

Alternately, you can play a literal game. The board game Monopoly, which gives players the chance to buy real estate and charge rent, can be enormously revealing in exposing a person's financial tendencies. Some people are noticeably conservative; they always want to keep plenty of money on hand, in case they have to pay another player. Other players take huge risks, spending every last dollar to build up real estate on their properties. It's a long game, and you'll learn a lot about the personalities—and financial priorities—of each of the players as it unfolds.

Our Draft of a Family Vision

Most families form their Family Vision through a variety of experiences—they have conversations, build values-based traditions, and share stories. That's been our experience as well—for our family, the vision plays out on a day-to-day basis like a mosaic. The different pieces come together through sharing "teachable moment" family stories, collectively deciding how to give to charity, volunteering together, and spending on meaningful experiences.

It's rare that people write down a formal Family Vision, but—once again, "the Harley factor" made us want to formalize our Vision so that our children and generations to come could read it. This Family Vision isn't meant to be read every day; rather, it's meant to serve a specific purpose as an anchor, useful especially during "stormy" times of transition or upheaval. When we formalized our Family Vision in writing, it reads as follows:

"Money is a tool, which enables us to save, enjoy, and give. We *save* so that we can achieve financial security and reach our highest potential, through pursuing education. We *enjoy* money as we experience a good quality of life, improved healthcare, and pursue meaningful experiences for our family. We *give* through volunteering our time, money, and by pushing ourselves to realize our full potential so that we can give back to the broader community. We also *give* by focusing on our obligation to future generations, ensuring that our children and grandchildren are protected, have financial literacy, and a clear vision for handling wealth."

Some families may arrive at a totally different Vision than ours. Their shared conclusion may be that money is meant to be enjoyed, especially on shared experiences. Other families may be intent on scrimping and saving, so that financial security is never in question. That's okay. What matters most is that families come together to have this conversation, so that there's shared trust and communication about where they're going, and how they're going to get there. Family history and awareness of sacrifice is the most important inheritance.

VALUES: FAMILY STEWARDSHIP

Out of vision grow values. Think of a tree: the vision forms the roots out of which grow the values and behaviors that come into visible fruition. The values that you and your family choose to emphasize in teachable moments will all be rooted in your vision for your family: one leads to the next.

We're going to assume that anyone reading this book has one component of their family vision in common: the desire to *pass on* wealth, values, and financial smarts. Although we're going to spend much of our subsequent chapters giving you ideas for how you can engender good financial values, we want to start by discussing a foundational concept which is critical for success in passing it on. This value informs all the other values we'll discuss: family stewardship.

Family stewards are motivated by a healthy obligation to care for future generations. They view their money not as a personal possession, but as a trust; they understand that their role is to maintain it, grow it, and pass it on to others. Their family vision for wealth stretches far into the future—it includes not just their children, but the multiple generations that will follow. In other words, family stewards have decided to play the long game.

We work with one woman who will inherit a large estate. In spite of what's coming to her, she still works professionally. She lives in a modest home and has taught her kids to live within their means. Instead of planning how she'll spend her millions, she's coming to us with questions about the best ways to perpetuate the money for her own kids and grandchildren. That's her version of family stewardship.

Successful family stewards must function as **family leaders**. Imagine that you raise your child to be values-driven and financially smart. You also raise them with a clear vision for the family wealth. As they enter adulthood and get married, though, they could still be overridden by their spouse; that's why it's so key to make sure they understand their role as leaders within their families.

This might seem like an oversimplification of what are often complicated family dynamics. Still, if you raise your children with vision, values, a sense of obligation to future generations, *and* an expectation for family leadership—that's a great place for any next generation to start.

Family stewardship is characterized by three main qualities:

1. Their financial habits are guided by **long-term financial goals**. These goals are determined by the family vision and by concern for future generations.
2. They are **financially literate**; they understand how to use financial strategies to cultivate the family estate and carry out the family vision.
3. They live with **gratitude and generosity**, stewarding not only their money, but also their time and talents.

If any family should be considered a case study in financial stewardship, it would have to be the Rockefellers. John D. Rockefeller, the family's patriarch, made his fortune through Standard Oil. His mother, a deeply religious Baptist, had taught her son to tithe 10 percent of everything he ever made—and he did. As one of our nation's first billionaires, Rockefeller became known for his philanthropy.

That legacy of paying it forward has formed the bedrock of the Rockefellers' family vision.[6] John D. Rockefeller had a mantra, which is now literally set in stone at Rockefeller Center in New York City: "For every right implies a responsibility; every opportunity, an obligation; every possession, a duty."[7] Their family vision focuses on their duty

6   "The Rockefellers: A Legacy of Giving." Rockefeller Philanthropy Advisors. Accessed May 23, 2019. https://www.rockpa.org/guide/rockefellers-legacy-giving/.

7   Frank, Robert. "4 Secrets to Raising Wealthy Kids, According to the Billionaire Rockefeller Family." CNBC. March 28, 2018. Accessed May 23, 2019. https://www.cnbc.com/2018/03/26/david-rockefeller-jr-shares-4-secrets-to-wealth-and-family.html.

to help others; their value of family stewardship grows out of that vision.

Gratitude and giving continue to characterize the Rockefeller heirs. One Rockefeller descendant, Michael Quattrone, described the legacy he'd been given by his predecessors. He said, "[I've received] the gift of inheriting a philanthropic tradition while being empowered to make it my own."[8] Quattrone expresses gratitude, not for his family's *wealth*, but for their *philanthropic tradition*. He also identifies his own vision for the future: Quattrone wants to carry the legacy on.

The Rockefellers are *stewards* of big wealth. They operate under the assumption that it's their job to handle their money well, and pass it on. The three qualities that characterize family stewardship are all easily recognizable in their legacy: they operate with long-term goals, determined by the family vision; they have continued to invest their money wisely, thanks to financial literacy and the help of expert guidance; and they live with clear gratitude and generosity.

Family stewardship can't happen without those values for giving and generosity. And, let's be honest: giving to others needs to be taught. It doesn't come naturally. What *does* come naturally? Selfishness. This point is made abundantly clear to anyone who spends time watching toddlers interact with cries of, "Mine! Mine! Mine!" If we're not trained to put the needs of others before our own—to share, to

---

8   Sullivan, Paul. "Giving Like a Rockefeller, Even If You're Not Super-Rich." The New York Times. March 31, 2017. Accessed May 23, 2019. https://www.nytimes.com/2017/03/31/your-money/david-rockefeller-philanthropy.html.

give, to sacrifice—it can be easy to conclude that the world revolves around us.

We're going to spend much of the rest of our book discussing the first two characteristics of family stewardship: long-term goal setting and financial literacy. The third characteristic is worth discussing in greater depth now: gratitude and giving.

EMPHASIZE GRATITUDE AND GIVING

In 2013, a story about the "Affluenza teen" made headlines. The teen, a young man named Ethan Couch, killed four people when he drunkenly drove his SUV onto the sidewalk. A psychologist testifying at his trial suggested that Couch didn't understand the consequences of his actions because he had "affluenza"—in other words, he was just too rich to know right from wrong.[9] People were furious about the suggestion that Couch be pitied and excused for being "too rich." Still—we can testify to the phenomenon that Couch represents. If kids aren't taught to think of other people, they will instinctively and mainly think of themselves. This can be especially true of children who grow up rich.

However, **giving and gratitude work as an antidote to entitlement.** We have many clients characterized by generosity and thankfulness, and they've got a bounce in their step. They've got a vision of giving, which helps

---

9   Roberts, Molly. "Ethan Couch Is a Very Convenient Target." The Washington Post. April 03, 2018. Accessed May 23, 2019. https://www.washingtonpost.com/blogs/post-partisan/wp/2018/04/03/the-affluenza-teen-is-an-easy-target/?noredirect=on&utm_term=.6d7f6207e5b6.

them handle their money with the next generation in mind. They're motivated to push their money into perpetuity, not just spend through it. They also demonstrate purpose, hope, and a sense of meaning.

For example, we saw our own children's sense of entitlement fade by participating in an act of generosity. Our children's school recently did a shoe drive to collect shoes for children in Africa. We watched our kids realize important truths about the world as they watched videos about the African children they were going to be helping, many of whom had to walk long distances to get fresh water. Our kids got excited and involved. They ransacked our closets and worked to get the shoes as clean as possible before donating them.

The shoe drive gave us new opportunities at home to talk with our kids about the ways we're blessed as a family. Before this drive, it's doubtful our children would have given a second thought to the fact that they always had shoes to wear. The act of giving opened their eyes to the needs of others and also helped them feel grateful for what they had. Moments like these open the door to revisit the Family Vision and establish values of family stewardship.

We want our kids to understand that the world is bigger than themselves. We want to demonstrate firsthand that it's better to give than receive. We want to ingrain the value that working to improve your community is part of what it means to be alive.

We believe that when children feel a sense of gratitude for what they've been given and are shown a vision for giving, they're far more likely to carry on a powerful sense of obligation to care for future generations.

And that sense of obligation? That's a game changer.

THE POWER OF OBLIGATION

Out of vision grow our values. Similarly, from the value of financial stewardship grows a sense of obligation that we should care for others and not just ourselves.

People's financial habits are often dictated most by what they feel a sense of obligation to. When this obligation is targeted in a healthy direction, as we'll recommend, your family's vision can be established for generations.

Many people function with no obligation. They trust that wealth is meant to be enjoyed, and they live large. From what we've seen in our work, and in discussions with colleagues, money is most often frittered away when there's *no* sense of obligation to future generations.

Equally problematic is financial behavior that's directed by the *wrong* obligation. Let's consider a hypothetical example of how this wrong obligation can often play out through the story of Tracy.

THE WRONG OBLIGATION

Tracy's dad was a hard worker, putting in over thirty years as a machinist at the same company. The company—we'll call it "ABC Inc."—had rewarded his years of hard work, granting him a pension and company stock.

Tracy grew up hearing her dad praise ABC Inc. When her dad said grace over their food at dinner, he'd mention his company by name. ABC Inc. had set him up with a comfortable retirement, thanks to his pension and the generous dividend checks which arrived.

When he passed away, Tracy inherited his stock. After years of steady growth, the stock had left her with sizable wealth, and she became as passionate a believer in the reliability of ABC Inc. as her father ever was. Her father had told her to never sell the ABC stock, but Tracy wouldn't have sold them anyway. Given how closely she associated the company with her father, selling the stock would have felt like selling a piece of him.

But the ABC stock wasn't as reliable as Tracy believed. When the financial crisis of 2008 hit, the price for ABC stock plummeted. News articles reported that ABC Inc. had over-extended themselves in credit. They'd become too big, too unwieldy, and were trying to branch out in too many directions.

Say Tracy came into our office at that point—a point at which ABC stock might have finally climbed back in a place where selling would be beneficial. We would urge Tracy to do what would have been the best strategy all along: diversify.

But Tracy says she just can't do that. ABC Inc. doesn't just amount to dollars and cents. ABC Inc., to Tracy, *is* her father. It's all those prayers said over the dinner table. It's every vacation she ever took, funded by the dividends checks. Tracy feels *loyal* to ABC Inc. to the same degree that she feels love for her father.

Tracy feels an obligation to a company, for understandable reasons. However, that sense of obligation leads to confusion about the best financial decision to make. In essence, a misdirected obligation can get in the way of making rational decisions based on fundamental data.

Industries and companies change. They've gotten more complex, and the right investment strategy for Tracy's dad is probably not the best investment strategy for Tracy's son. The wrong obligation can set you up for bad decision making. Instead of working to care for your future generations, you can easily end up losing the bulk of your estate entirely.

THE HEALTHIER OBLIGATION

Let us be clear: you *should* love and learn from your predecessors. It wasn't wrong for Tracy to appreciate the past, love her father, and want to honor him with how she handled the wealth he'd given her. Those emotions were entirely appropriate. However, Tracy misstepped when she put all of her focus into a company and attempted to maintain her father's *exact* financial strategy, without taking into account how that strategy might need to change to accommodate the changing times. A better way for her to honor his legacy would have been to perpetuate his wise financial stewardship.

We want to suggest that **the healthiest obligation you can feel, as a family steward of your wealth, is to *future generations.*** When families direct themselves with this healthy obligation, they are better equipped to build and perpetuate wealth, not mishandle or lose it. These families feel an obligation to pass the wealth onto others, specifically to future generations and through philanthropy.

Warren Buffett is an amazing example of what this looks like practically. Although he's one of the richest men in the world, he's lived a life characterized by generosity. His family has seen him give close to 90 billion dollars to charity, and he plans to leave the bulk of his estate to charity as well. His children won't be hung out to dry. In a letter he wrote to the Gates Foundation, Buffett wrote, "I want to give my kids just enough so that they would feel that they could do anything, but not so much that they would feel like doing nothing."[10] He has raised his kids to live modestly, teaching them that he doesn't measure his success by his money, but by how many people care about him. That's values-driven family stewardship.

When we got married and had kids, we felt a number of obligations. We wanted to love each other well and be good parents. We wanted to raise our kids to have upstanding values and become good members of society. We wanted to honor our parents and grandparents, carrying on their legacies and values. For us, all those obligations can come together when we focus on raising up the next generation well.

If part of your Family Vision recognizes an obligation to provide for the next generation, then work to instill values of family stewardship in your own kids. Help them live

10 Willett, Megan. "15 Tycoons Who Won't Leave Their Fortunes To Their Kids." Business Insider. Business Insider, August 20, 2013. https://www.businessinsider. com/tycoons-not-leaving-money-to-their-kids-2013-8#business-magnate-warren-buffett-1.

meaningful lives, characterized by kindness and generosity. Give them a vision to rally behind.

THE ROOTS OF A FRUITFUL TREE

Vision, values, and a healthy obligation come to define the families who are successful in passing it on.

Families don't often sit down to intentionally think through a Family Vision, values, and what—if anything—they should feel obligated to. However, when they do, the results are powerful:

- Vision: Families are able to form a core identity, which provides children with greater psychological resilience and inspiration for the future.
- Values: By working to live into the values of family stewardship, your kids will develop a focus that reaches beyond themselves and includes the care of other people. The value of family stewardship, as opposed to selfish spending, will better equip your kids to make wise financial decisions, and live lives of grateful giving.
- Obligation: By recognizing that we should feel *obligated* to invest in future generations, we set ourselves a clear long-term goal. This healthy obligation can clarify financial decisions and improve our financial strategy; it can also help us avoid making financial moves dictated by the wrong obligations.

As we learned with Anna and her quip about the rental house, the most important first step you can take is *communication*. Begin the conversation as a family—over dinner, on a walk, while eating ice cream, on a car ride—whenever you're gathered and in the mood for a good talk.

Get a sense of how each person would answer the question "What is money for?" Learn their priorities, and lead your family in forming a collective vision. Identify your goals. Consider what values you want to embrace as a family, and discuss what it means to be a family steward. Brainstorm your blessings to help stir up a sense of giving and gratitude.

The effect will be like planting good roots and watering the soil. This is just the beginning, but from it, the future will grow.

CHAPTER TWO

———

SHOW, SHARE, AND SURROUND

We generally change ourselves for one of two reasons: inspiration or desperation.

JIM ROHN

FINANCIAL INSPIRATION: ROGER NARRATES

As I've shared, financial trouble hit my family hard when I was around age ten. Whether we were trying to figure out what kind of car we could afford or weighing the cost of me going out for sports—we felt it. The financial stress was always there.

I was motivated by those experiences to seek out knowledge that would help me be more financially secure as an adult. But it wasn't just the *desperation* that motivated me—I also had moments of real financial *inspiration* too. Those memories are vivid in my brain, and I'm sure they stuck with me because they felt so powerful at the time.

One of the most powerful experiences came from simply witnessing what financial security could provide for a family. As a teenager, I worked full-time for my grandfather during the summers, helping him with his carpentry work. I got to know one of his regular clients, Bob. Bob was a company executive and lived in an enormous, beautifully crafted home. When he and his family prepared to leave for a long trip, he asked me if I would be willing to stay in his house and take care of it.

I jumped at the chance. I loved staying in Bob's beautiful home, and his influence opened my eyes to what was possible. Bob took amazing care of his family. He traveled the world. He paid me well for an experience that I would have done for free. He seemed secure, generous, and rarely seemed anxious.

Getting to know Bob also helped correct a wrong idea I'd always had about "rich people." Growing up, there was a common misperception in my community that rich people only had money because they'd gotten lucky. Many people even looked down on people with money as elitist. But, as I got to know Bob, I concluded that he didn't fit that category at all. It was obvious to me that his wealth had come from something much more substantial than just luck. He was a person whose values and intelligence I admired. Somehow, I concluded, he had helped *make* this happen. Perhaps, I thought, being wealthy was different from being "rich." As I observed Bob, I came up with a new definition for wealthy: to be wealthy is to know how to make smart, sound decisions that build upon and maintain your wealth for the long term.

Much of my future financial behaviors were formed before I

ever used a debit card. They were formed through *watching* adults around me and picking up lessons from them. Your children and grandchildren are no different. Regardless of how old they are, their financial habits will be largely influenced by what they see (or saw) from you as well as what they observe from the other major influences in their lives (like mentors, friends, and often spouses).

In this chapter, we'll discuss the lessons your children and grandchildren will pick up from watching you: some of their biggest influences. It's impossible to overestimate the influence you will wield on your children's financial behavior. We see the evidence of that influence with our clients every day.

We're going to talk about financial behaviors you can **show** your children and grandchildren so they're ultimately *inspired* to develop the financial habits and values you want them to have. Because you play the biggest role in shaping the financial perspectives of your kids and grandkids, we're going to devote the biggest section of this chapter to healthy financial habits you can model to them.

But, as we know, a parent is not their child's only influence. As we think about passing on wealth to future generations, it's also critical to **share** stories about the generations that have gone before. By connecting the dots for your kids about how wealth was built, you will better equip them to carry on a Family Vision and practice the habits of a wealth-builder.

Finally, it's also important to think about the other influencers who shape your younger family members. **Surround** your children with people who can help model good financial behaviors, and live out values like giving to others. We'll also discuss how to mitigate the potential negative influences that might come from key players in their lives. I am a strong believer in Jim Rohn's theory that you are the average of the five people you spend the most time with.[11] Bob pulled up my average and I have become mindful of whom I surround my own children with as I know it will heavily influence their value system and their views on money.

SHOW

Imagine you're a twelve-year-old kid whose parents live in a mansion they were given by your grandmother. Neither parent works. They mostly watch TV or hang out by the pool. When they feel like a shift in pace, they buy something—new clothes, new furniture, a new pet.

If you were to grow up witnessing that influence, you wouldn't have any understanding of how the world of economics works. Money would seem to be always available in abundance. You would simply expect it to fall off trees, and you would spend it in that fashion.

Kids understand how the world works by observing their parents. You can spend years telling your kids to say "please" and "thank you," but they probably won't say either unless they hear you saying the same thing regularly. Similarly, if your kids perceive that money comes freely from wealthy

---

11   Groth, Aimee. "You're The Average Of The Five People You Spend The Most Time With." Business Insider. Business Insider, July 24, 2012. https://www.businessinsider.com/jim-rohn-youre-the-average-of-the-five-people-you-spend-the-most-time-with-2012-7.

relatives and requires no work on their parents' end, that will be their expectation as an adult. They'll act accordingly. But, if they see their parents and major adult influencers as *participators* in the world economy, they'll better understand that they need to be active participants themselves.

You can help your children understand key lessons about economics, about where money comes from, and about the importance of our own effort and investment, by demonstrating **a strong work ethic**. In doing so, you'll help teach your children how to invest in their community and work for a cause bigger than themselves.

Both of us feel that our own parents did a great job of modeling a good work ethic to us as kids. Lori's parents both worked full-time jobs, and they never complained about work or pretended to call in sick. Even outside of work, they were still productive with their time, whether that was gardening, landscaping, or helping the church. Likewise, Roger's parents were always gainfully employed. No matter the weather or how they were feeling, they, too, did what they had to do to make ends meet for their family.

Many of our clients are in a position where they don't actually need to be gainfully employed to enjoy a comfortable living. That's okay—you can still show your kids a strong work ethic by demonstrating your investment in the things that you care about. Whether that's volunteering at the local school, serving on charity boards, caring for a garden, or what have you—there is tremendous value in modeling productivity and hard work to your kids.

In order for kids to grow up into adults who are capable of

passing on the family wealth, they need to understand that wealth requires effort—to build, to maintain, and to track. It's less likely that they will be eager to work hard for the good of their family if they don't see their main influencers allocating their time productively.

Teaching your kids to work hard is one of the most powerful traits you can model to them, and it will play a major factor in how successful they are at practicing the other three traits we recommend you show your kids and that are components of our Family Vision: **save, enjoy,** and **give**.

SHOW HOW TO SAVE

The saying, "shirtsleeves to shirtsleeves" describes a depressing concept. The expression means that a fortune won't last beyond three generations. The first generation will roll up their shirtsleeves to build wealth; the second generation will enjoy the wealth in gowns and suit jackets; the third generation will lose it, and once more have to roll up their shirtsleeves to work.

Why would this be? Typically, wealth *builders* conduct themselves according to financially savvy values: they save, they budget, and they shrewdly negotiate and manage their money. That's how they establish a fortune. As they raise the second generation, they'll pass on some of these values to their children, but the values won't have the same immediacy that they did for their parents. When kids grow up experiencing a level of comfort and wealth, it can feel less necessary to save and budget.

Then, along comes the third generation. If the second generation isn't highly motivated to pass on the values they learned from their parents, the third generation may be characterized by lavish spending and a sense of entitlement. The values that helped their family build wealth fall by the wayside. It's that generation—the saying goes—that will end up losing the family wealth.

This "shirtsleeves to shirtsleeves" concept is a pattern that we've witnessed firsthand. It's certainly not the rule—we know many families who do successfully pass on their wealth and a sense of obligation to future generations. Still, it happens a lot. If you want to make your wealth last and perpetuate your values, we believe one of the most important steps a family can take is to pass on the values that built the wealth in the first place.

How do you begin? Model the importance of **saving** to your kids. Saving behaviors can have more impact on wealth than even income or investing, mainly due to the effects of compounding interest. There are hundreds of amazing stories about "working class benefactors," like janitors, secretaries, or grocers, who were able to leave millions to charity, mainly because they were such diligent savers.[12] On the other hand, there are also countless stories of people who gained sudden wealth through an NFL contract, lottery win, or inheritance, and ended up needing to declare bankruptcy only a few years later.[13] The contrast in these scenarios makes one thing clear: perpetual wealth—wealth

---

12 LaBianca, Juliana. "These People Donated Millions After They Died-But No One Knew They Were Rich." Reader's Digest. May 20, 2019. Accessed August 10, 2019. https://www.rd.com/true-stories/inspiring/secret-millionaires-donations-after-died/.

13 Fox, Michelle. "Inside the NY Giants Money Boot Camp: How to Tackle Some Wild Spending Habits." CNBC. CNBC, September 30, 2019. https://www.cnbc.com/2019/09/27/inside-the-ny-giants-money-boot-camp.html.

that lasts through multiple generations — is built on a *savings* mentality.

We're not advocating for extreme savings or thrift; we know those can come with an emotional price tag. Extreme savings can also ultimately be a fool's errand: it can deprive you from living life fully. However, we do recognize that successful families appear to have found a balance between sacrifice and pleasure. Adult children in these successful families have taken up the shared Family Vision, kept the family's long-term targets in mind, and still allow short term emotions to move in their natural cycles. They're values-driven, and financially smart.

If you want to raise kids who are disciplined at saving money, help them maintain the long view of family stewardship — to be thoughtful of their own futures, and even the futures of their own children. These values will help them navigate their own emotions as they weigh whether to save or spend. Specifically, you can help model habits of saving by focusing on values like **cost consciousness** and **delayed gratification.**

Saving via Cost Consciousness

We heard a story of a celebrity athlete who made approximately $100 million over the course of his career. He finally sought out a financial advisor after his fortune shrank to ten million. He gave his advisor all of his account statements and a paper history of his business dealings, seeking the answer to one main question: "Have I been getting ripped off?"

This athlete had seen 90 million dollars evaporate because

he'd stopped paying attention to where his money was going. He hadn't paid attention to the dollar amount of a good deal versus a bad deal. He may not have done his homework about the trustworthiness of the people he employed. He wasn't conscious of the cost of doing business. Cost consciousness just didn't seem necessary—until, all of a sudden, it was.

Such a high dollar figure—$100 million—may seem like an infinite amount of money, but it's not. Even enormous estates can plunge into bankruptcy when handled thoughtlessly, and it happens often enough that we have proverbs like, "shirtsleeves to shirtsleeves." Wealth builders are **cost conscious**. They make sure that they get their money's worth.

Getting accustomed to wealth can make us lose cost consciousness. When money in the bank feels guaranteed, we can become thoughtless. We stop paying attention to the little things, and money gets frittered away. It's this thoughtlessness that's cured when we value cost consciousness: we're more thoughtful and purposeful about where our money goes.

So how do you show kids the value of being cost conscious? Show them your own thoughtfulness about where your money goes. Teach them to compare prices at the grocery store. Grow vegetables in the summer. Show your kids how to look for a good deal. Take advantage of sales.

When kids are shown that money can be saved here or there, they understand that money is not limitless. They learn it's important to be thoughtful about where the money goes. If they understand that, they're in a much better position than they would be otherwise to pass on wealth of their own.

Saving via Delayed Gratification

"Lori, there's a Starbucks. Do you want to stop and get something?"

"Hm… Do I want a vanilla latte, or do I want to retire?"

Some version of this quip comes up often between the two of us, but joking aside, we know how easy it is to fritter away money at the expense of achieving long-term goals. Ideally, we want our kids to avoid that pitfall and develop the discipline needed to save toward long-term goals. This discipline requires **delayed gratification**, one of the defining characteristics of a successful family steward.

At seven years old, Will is at an age where he is constantly spotting things he'd like to buy—especially LEGO sets. However, Will also wants to save for a dirt bike. We try to press him to really think about those impulse buys. We know that he's going to experience less and less satisfaction with each impulsive purchase, whereas if we can teach him to delay gratification, he's going to be set up for success in many areas of life. So, when he asks—we talk.

"Will, do you really need another LEGO set? Or do you want to keep saving your money for a dirt bike?"

Sometimes, he'll shrug and agree that his baby brother would be likely to lose or ruin the LEGO set anyway. By asking little questions during purchasing time, or when our kids receive money, we're trying to show them that saving for big ticket items (or simply saving to build up cash) requires discipline and delayed gratification. In the same way we regularly emphasize the importance of education or kindness, we're trying to make financial thoughtfulness a theme of our kids' lives.

There's a famous study called "The Marshmallow Experiment" that helped people realize how important habits of delayed gratification can be in determining success. In the study, conducted by Walter Mischell at Stanford University, children were seated at a table and a marshmallow was placed in front of them. They were told that the experimenter was going to leave them alone in the room, and they had two options about what they could do with that tempting marshmallow. One option: they could choose to ring a bell at any time to call the experimenter back into the room, and then eat the marshmallow. Their second option: they could *wait* until the experimenter returned and then get two marshmallows.

Some kids took the immediate reward. Other kids practiced delayed gratification; they waited and then received a bigger reward. Decades later, Mischel managed to track down fifty-nine of the original test subjects, who were now all in their forties. A self-control test was administered to the group, and for the most part, the same subjects that practiced delayed gratification as children also showed strong will power as an adult.[14]

---

14 "Delaying Gratification." What You Need to Know About Will-Power: the Psychological Science of Self-Control. American Psychological Association. Accessed October 28, 2019. https://www.apa.org/helpcenter/willpower-gratification. pdf.

There have been many arguments made against the marshmallow test, but our professional and personal experience confirms that Mischel's results are more telling than we want to believe. Among our clients, we see habits of delayed gratification leading to successful, long-term health and financial behavior. When people struggle to delay gratification, that's when we more often see financial missteps. These impressions echo the results that were discovered in a more recent study, published by the National Bureau of Economic Research.

The test surveyed older Americans using the question: If you were offered $100 right now, or could wait a year for a higher amount, how much more money would it take for you to wait a year? If someone demanded a higher dollar amount, they would be considered less patient. The study's findings concluded that the least-patient people had significantly lower net worth. The study writers inferred that these impatient people likely had saved less and had fewer assets in their later years. Not only that, these less-patient people were less likely to take care of their bodies with healthy habits, or to plan for future life challenges. On the other hand, people who showed more patience ended up with better health, contingency plans, and higher net worth.

Clearly, a key quality to being able to pass it on from one generation to the next is this ability to *delay* gratification. In fact, one of the reasons we have the lifestyle values we do is because of a generational lesson that was passed down to Lori from her father about this very concept. Whenever Lori's dad wanted anything when he was younger, big or small, his father always used to say: "Wait two weeks and see if you still want it." The "wait two weeks" advice created some frustration at times, but it also ingrained an appreciation for delayed gratification which has helped us in countless ways.

For people who want to build or maintain wealth, delayed gratification is crucial. Most of the rewards in the wealth-building process involve waiting. We wait for the stock market to steadily trend upwards; we wait for interest to compound; we wait for real estate to gain equity. The gratification comes after long delays.

So, how can you show delayed gratification to your own children and grandchildren? As parents now, we've adopted this nugget of wisdom from Lori's grandfather in our own parenting. We'll often force a pause between our kids' expressed desire for something and when we end up buying it (if we do), sometimes even chiming in with the same phrase Lori's grandfather always did: "Wait two weeks, and then tell us if you still want it." Nine times out of ten, they forget about what they ask for within minutes. If they won't stop talking about something, that's when we know they truly want it.

You can also help show delayed gratification by talking with your kids about your own habits of waiting and working toward a goal. Working out, planning for the future, eating nutritiously—those are all habits of delayed gratification that you can point out to your kids.

We can't stress enough how valuable it is to teach delayed gratification to your children and grandchildren. Building habits of delayed gratification will help your kids not only avoid impulse buying, but also help ingrain a long-term wealth building mindset—and even more wide-reaching habits of health and future planning.

SHOW HOW TO ENJOY: LORI NARRATES

We've talked about ways to show your children and grand-children habits of saving—now, we want to talk about showing them *enjoyment* of your hard work.

Kids need to experience firsthand the rewards that come from saving up and making sacrifices for their long-term goals—otherwise, what's the point? We've tried a number of ways to show our kids the rewarding experiences that can come when we spend with intention. We've pursued music lessons, joined adult hockey teams, taken family ski trips, enjoyed time at a cabin property, and are working on a goal to visit all fifty states before Anna graduates.

Likewise, we love celebrating with our kids when they successfully save up for something and finally realize they have enough to buy their big-ticket item. That's when our kids realize that this awesome new purchase was made possible by their hard work. We want them to enjoy every bit of the payoff!

Recently, I took the kids to Dick's Sporting Goods. Will has become obsessed with our Milwaukee basketball team, The Bucks, and has asked on various occasions to buy something Bucks related. We have continued to employ our "wait two weeks" strategy, guessing he would eventually lose interest, but Will's Bucks fervor has held firm. On this recent trip to Dick's, Will's eyes grew wide when he saw all the different Bucks apparel hung up—especially when he saw the one with his favorite player's name: Giannis Antetokounmpo. He immediately began begging to get it.

Since Will had outlasted our "wait two weeks" strategy, I tried a different tack. "Can you buy that with your own money, Will?" I asked.

"Yes!" he said. "I have twenty dollars saved from my allowance, and you owe me two!" Leave it to Will to remember that we owe him money.

"Well, let's think about it," I said. "We'll put the t-shirt in the cart and we can just think about it while we do the rest of our shopping." Halfway through our shopping trip, I reminded Will about his dirt bike goal. "You'd be giving up money for your dirt bike if you got this t-shirt, bud." That prompted reflection from my seven year old. He really wants that dirt bike.

However, by the time we got to the register, Will was just as exuberant about the t-shirt as when he first saw it. We talked through the purchase and he concluded this was something he wanted to spend his money on.

Talk about enjoyment: for weeks after that shopping trip, Will's love for this t-shirt was unmistakable. He never wanted to take it off! Roger and I had to laugh when we saw him come down the stairs with it on, every single morning. Obviously, this was a worthwhile splurge for him, and we were delighted to see him enjoy it so much.

This enjoyment matters, and it extends far beyond just fun splurges, like vacations or new t-shirts. By working hard to build wealth, you can also *enjoy* good health, because you have access to the best healthcare. You can *enjoy* a great education, and set yourself up to make an amazing contribution to the world. You can *enjoy* peace of mind, through establishing financial security.

As you express your own gratitude for the financially strong position you might be in, let your kids hear how thankful you are for all the different benefits you enjoy!

SHOW HOW TO GIVE: LORI NARRATES

We discussed the importance of giving and gratitude in our previous chapter. How can you instill those values in your kids? *Show* them that it's something you personally value.

I'm on a committee which gives out scholarship money for high-school girls to attend college. Every year, when the scholarship applications flood in, I spend much of my evenings reading over the essays, which naturally prompts questions from our kids about what I'm doing. I explain to the kids how the scholarship applications work, why I volunteered to help, and how I decide who should get the money. The kids understand that I'm spending my evenings helping other people go to college.

Sometimes, modeling our value for giving gets a little awkward. For instance, Roger and I give a percentage of our earnings to our church, via electronic donation. However, it occurred to us recently that our kids weren't *seeing* that act of giving. For all they knew, we were showing up to church every Sunday and making absolutely no investment in the church's programs that were benefiting us. Plus, we were urging them to give some of their allowance money—but they weren't seeing us do the same thing. I concluded that somehow, we had to get them a visual of our online giving.

One Sunday morning, as the offering bucket started being passed, I had a sudden inspiration. I grabbed an offering envelope which had a box marked "I give online." I checked the box, flashed the envelope to Anna and Will, and dropped it in the offering basket as it passed.

The kids looked at me skeptically. They're not so young they can't tell the difference between their cold, hard cash, and my empty envelope. "Why did you do that?" Will asked.

"I wanted you guys to see that we give too," I whispered back. "I checked the box. Did you see?"

"Yeah, but it's *empty*," Will said. I shushed him. How could I explain that I wanted him to have a visual of this value? On the ride home, we picked up the conversation and were able to discuss the idea more fully.

Some of these efforts to model good financial habits may feel awkward or forced. Still, we think the efforts are worth it. If nothing else, they'll help prompt conversation which will give you an opportunity to explain to your kids what you care about. As they grow up seeing you actively working to give back to others, they'll come to understand that's a valuable experience for them to have too.

SHARE

We've talked about financial behaviors you can *show* to your kids. Perhaps equally important is *sharing* stories with them that will help them form their sense of identity and values within your family. It's also valuable to share life-lessons which will help build your kids' financial smarts.

SHARING FAMILY STORIES: ROGER NARRATES

When I was growing up, I heard countless stories about how the farm property owned by my family had provided for us over the years. At age thirteen, my grandfather took over running the farm after his father died. He took care of the livestock, grew hay to be sold, and helped maintain an enormous garden which provided their staple foods growing up. Now, my uncle puts in the work required to maintain the family farm. While chopping wood or haying with my uncle, I would hear about how generations of their family benefitted from the farm property. Now, I'm telling these stories to my own kids to help them appreciate their history and the value of hard work.

This practice of sharing family stories, as it turns out, is a major commonality in families who successfully pass on wealth for multiple generations. In an interview with David Rockefeller Jr., he was asked for some of the secrets of how his family has maintained such wealth over so many generations. The first answer he gave was regular family meetings. He explained that the entire Rockefeller clan meets twice a year, often over the holidays, for family meetings, starting at age twenty-one. Rockefeller calls them the "family forums," and they include spouses that have married into the family. At these forums, the family discusses its vision for the future, projects, new additions to the family either via marriage or birth, and other big family news items. They seek to make everyone there feel closely connected to the family, even those that have joined by marriage.[15]

An article discussing Rockefeller's interview notes: "Rockefeller says it's also important to *maintain family history*. The Rockefellers do this in part via their family 'homesteads,' where they can gather and connect with their past. 'It's places that were familiar and that were passed down over generations,' he said. 'I can go back to the place where my great grandfather lived over 100 years ago and see how he lived and see how his son and their grandchildren lived.'"[16]

The Rockefellers are known for their success in passing on their Family Vision and the values of family stewardship from generation to generation—and one of the biggest tools they use to do it is *sharing* family history. They spend time with one another regularly, review the Family Vision, and help family members understand the history that has led to their success and perpetuated wealth. The fact that they meet at these family homesteads means they're giving their younger family members clear visuals of the history and values that paved the way for their family's success.

The more tangible you can make your family's history, the better. We know one client who brings along his children and grandchildren to the original buildings he bought when he was just starting out. He even shows them some of his

---

15 Frank, Robert. "4 Secrets to Raising Wealthy Kids, According to the Billionaire Rockefeller Family." CNBC. March 28, 2018. Accessed August 12, 2019. https://www.cnbc.com/2018/03/26/david-rockefeller-jr-shares-4-secrets-to-wealth-and-family.html.

16 Ibid, our emphasis

first delivery trucks. There's a review of the blood, sweat, and sacrifices that were put in by their ancestors.

When children from wealthy families hear these stories, their understanding of money changes. It goes from something they may have always had in abundance, to something that's connected to hard work and sacrifice. That, in turn, changes how they use it. They're more likely to become family stewards and connect to a larger Family Vision than simply spend right through it.

For example, I feel a sense of accountability toward my great-grandparents, who started the farm, and my grandfather and uncle, who have preserved it. A hayfield quickly becomes overgrown if it isn't maintained, and it takes incredible work to do so. Because I know how much time, effort, and energy goes into preserving the farm, I feel a high level of accountability to be thoughtful about the money it provides.

We witness the change in our clients' behavior when they know the family stories. In our business, it's common for people to give thousands of dollars a year to each of their children as a way to help and potentially avoid estate tax on that money, later on. Many adult children come to rely on this money as part of their income; they have ideas of how they want to spend it even before it hits their bank accounts. But the children who are more connected to their family history operate differently. When that $15,000 feels connected to hard work and sacrificial family members, we see clients being more thoughtful about how they invest those gifts.

It's important to note that stories don't just help kids on the financial level. It also helps them on a deep, psychological level. Children who grow up hearing stories of their family history have been shown to be more resilient and mentally strong, than those who haven't.

The *New York Times* published a story called "The Family Stories that Bind Us in This Life."[17] In the article, they mentioned a "Do You Know?" (DYK) scale, which is a list of twenty questions that children would only know the answers to if they'd been told family stories. For instance, one of the questions is, "Do you know how your parents met?" Or, "Do you know the names of the schools your parents attended?" The only way a child would have an answer to those questions is if there had been conversations about family history.

In a follow-up blog to the original article, Marshall P. Duke, PhD., professor of Psychology at Emory University explained, "…higher scores on the DYK scale were associated with higher levels of self-esteem, an internal locus of control (a belief in one's own capacity to control what happens to him or her), better family functioning, lower levels of anxiety, fewer behavioral problems, and better chances for good outcomes if a child faces educational or emotional/behavioral difficulties."[18]

---

17 Feiler, Bruce. "The Stories That Bind Us." *The New York Times*. March 15, 2013. Accessed August 12, 2019. https://www.nytimes.com/2013/03/17/fashion/the-family-stories-that-bind-us-this.life.html.

18 Duke, Marshall P., PhD. "The Stories That Bind Us: What Are the Twenty Questions?" HuffPost. May 23, 2013. Accessed August 12, 2019. https://www.huffpost.com/entry/the-stories-that-bind -us_b_2918975?guccounter=1&guce_referrer=aHRocHM6Ly93d3cuZ29vZ2xlLmNvbS8S8&guce_referrer_sig=AQAAAItAPfW20i9RJbWPR-TxcQcMfhz20c7s_dKUuIWEtGHIW4j3koXOqR3lYhAcTBE8iUqTiQiul8r0_o6oxoiDscFLODTlM1c-9UMTooj_lDw7bEwx78Tv5iDmNy1LozLMa73vEXMAGB9LRD35v1N7R7UTEpLavMxfwxx9jwALTdX_.

That's profound! Children with a strong sense of their family history were shown to be far more psychologically strong than those that had less understanding of their family history.

However, it's not enough to simply hand your kids a list of answers to these twenty questions and make sure they memorize them. What makes families successful who pass along the answers to these questions is *time together* and *conversation*. Kids in these families know the answers to the questions, because there's regular storytelling and time spent together as a family, during meals, vacations, and holidays. Think back to the Rockefellers' method of their family forums twice a year. They're not just making announcements or discussing their Family Vision via shared emails—they're spending time together, and talking face-to-face.

This chapter's goal is to offer ways you can help your kids take up the values represented in your Family Vision. Modeling good financial habits and values is one step. Helping your kids build up their core identity through family togetherness and sharing stories is another big step toward passing on the Family Vision.[19]

One last important note in sharing stories about your family's history: don't just share the happy stuff. Share about the hard moments too. Research shows that families are more successful when they share both the ups and downs

19 Duke, Marshall P. "The Stories That Bind Us: What Are the Twenty Questions?" HuffPost. HuffPost, May 23, 2013. https://www.huffpost.com/entry/the-stories-that-bind-us-_b_2918975.

in their storytelling.[20] When talking about family history, some people might only want to share the positive memories. However, that gives your kids an impression that, when *they* inevitably hit a hard time, they're alone in going through it. They won't have any sense that other people in their family have had to get through similar struggles. However, if they have heard stories of their ancestors getting through hard times, they know there's a precedent to enduring and ultimately coming out the other side.

We've observed the truth of this in our clients. The children who have grown up with an understanding of their ancestors' struggles, efforts—even failures—are generally more thoughtful about how they use their money. That money feels weighty with their family's sacrifices, and they're considerate about how they steward it. On the other hand, children who grow up with the idea that their family has always had it easy, seem less motivated to provide for their own future generations.

Ideally, we want our own kids to maintain humility and gratitude while leveraging the privilege of family wealth to live purposeful lives. For that ideal to play out, we know they need to feel a sense of obligation toward the previous generation's sacrifice—they need to hear the stories about everything our parents and grandparents did to help us get to where we are now. They also need to feel an obligation to preserve tangible family unity, like what we've experienced via Roger's family farm. Lastly, they need to feel an obliga-

---

20 Fivush, Robyn, Marshall Duke, and Jennifer G. Bohanek. "Do You Know: The Power of Family History in Adolescent Identity and Well-Being." National Council on Public History. Emory University, February 23, 2010. https://ncph.org/wp-content/uploads/2013/12/The-power-of-family-history-in-adolescent-identity.pdf.

tion to contribute to the family wealth, so that their own children and grandchildren can enjoy the same privileges.

To get them there—we need to share our stories.

SHARING LESSONS: LORI NARRATES

It's also valuable to share nuggets of advice with your children and grandchildren about how the world works, as a step toward building up their financial smarts. Do your best to let these conversations come up naturally, embracing "teachable moments" as the topic of money intersects with living life.

When I was a teenager, my dad would review the phone bill each month with my siblings and me. He would highlight which long distance calls were mine and point out the ones that belonged to my brother and sister. Each of us then needed to pay our "bill." On one occasion, I didn't have enough money to pay my bill! I remember being relieved when the punishment seemed minor—I simply couldn't use the phone until I paid up—but that punishment turned out to more painful than I expected! Those calls hadn't originally felt like a financial decision, but my dad helped me connect the dots between my actions and the financial reality. It was a memorable lesson!

Here and there, we're trying to help our kids connect the dots from their everyday experiences to financial implications. We've had lots of conversations with Anna about our rental house, which has provided her with a very elementary understanding about real estate investments, rental income, investing in our neighborhood community, and so on. When our kids get excited about a business like Under Armour or Disney, we tell them they could own stock in those companies one day.

In having these conversations, we're trying to show our kids that we can be thoughtful about every part of life. Whether we're eating, drinking, going to the store, or paying a phone bill, we can be intentional about how we interact with everything we see. Rather than just go through the motions, we're trying to share lessons about how the world goes around and comes together. Slowly, we're seeing our kids connect the dots on their own and improve as problem-solvers.

SURROUND

When the two of us think of some of our formative financial experiences, we can recall the people outside our parents that impacted us: people like Bob, who let Roger stay in his beautiful home. Mr. Talbott was the teacher in high-school who first gave Roger a worksheet to illustrate the power of compound interest. Lori can remember the female stockbroker who influenced her to become a financial advisor, and her work mentor, Barbara Sweeney, who invested countless hours helping her hone her skills. We can think of aunts, uncles, and grandparents who passed on stories and modeled values.

We were surrounded by some great people, and we know that the power of influence is strong among the people who surround your children and grandchildren. Clients regularly have told us stories about how influential their aunts, uncles, and grandparents have been in teaching them about investments. Some clients had relatives buy them their first stock, and others tagged along on appointments to meet with a stockbroker. Those influencers introduced our clients to the world of investing much earlier than most kids encounter it.

What does this mean to you? Pay attention to the people who surround your kids, and try to introduce them to good influences. Consider: What values are they absorbing from their best friends' families? From your neighbors? From their relatives? Although our kids are too young to be dating, we know that eventually they'll be heavily influenced by their boyfriends or girlfriends, or spouses, or in-laws. Are those influences positive or negative?

When looking for people to bring into your kids' lives, consider their values and behavior. Ideally, look for people who can uphold the values you want your kids to possess. As your kids get into high-school and college, they may also benefit from meeting family friends and acquaintances in various areas of the financial world, such as:

- Entrepreneurs,
- Certified Public Accountants (CPAs),
- Successful business leaders,
- Financial advisors, or
- Banking professionals.

Familiarity with each of these professions is going to give your kids a leg up. These areas of finance won't feel abstract and intimidating; they'll feel familiar and associated with a likable person. In high school, Lori shadowed people who ran successful businesses, which greatly impacted how she thought about her life goals and ambitions. After being introduced to her parents' CPA, she worked at their office for a tax season. Both experiences gave her more confidence to pursue her eventual career as a financial advisor.

As your kids get older, and especially after they finish high school and college, we believe it can be valuable to bring them along to financial advisor appointments. A financial advisor shouldn't be intimidating for kids. Instead, that person should be a real and important part of their lives.

One couple that we work with brought in their son when he was in high school. His grandmother had given him $10,000, and his parents thought it was a good moment for him to get to know us and have a conversation on ways to invest his money. We took the time to educate him on his choices, provide a foundational understanding of investing, and demonstrate how a financial advisor relationship would work. Other clients bring in their kids or grandkids when they've gotten their first high school job and need help understanding budgeting and planning. Sometimes, we see younger members of the family for the first time when they get their first career job and want to discuss how to set up their 401(k). These milestone moments can be a great opportunity to introduce trusted financial influences to your kids or grandkids, and provide some financial education.

Starting from high school, it's valuable for kids to learn about some of the financial literacy concepts we're going to discuss in the chapters to come. As your kids enter college, we recommend they start gathering a more formal financial team around them, possibly with your help. It's important that the people you introduce them to are capable and trustworthy. Refer to our Appendix for more specific suggestions on what qualifications to look for in these financial team members.

SPOUSAL INFLUENCE

When your kids are young and still in your home, there's no question that you as their parents/guardians will be their main influence. We can say with just as much confidence that if they grow up and get married, their biggest influence will be their spouse.

For some people, this is a terrifying thought. Attorneys have shared with us, if they truly want to motivate clients to update their estate plans, all they need to do is pose the prospect of how much money their daughter-in-law or son-in-law will get under their current plan. Often, the thought of their in-law getting a large portion of their estate is a scary enough thought that they'll jump into action.

When your children get married, they're tying their lives to another person, another set of financial experiences—another lifetime's worth of values. It can feel scary to imagine your money being handled by someone who possesses a value system that might be much different than your own.

As a parent, you could do everything right, but your kids might still have an independent streak and choose to disregard your advice. They might be influenced by a peer or a spouse who pulls them in a different direction. How do you prevent that negative influence?

We believe the answer is financial literacy. If you have provided your children with a clear understanding of how money works, of how investments work, of how compound interest works, and any number of other concepts—then they can be their own financial leaders. While they still might be influenced by a person with less financial literacy, they'll have a clearer understanding of what might happen to their finances if they take the other person's advice. They'll be more confident in conversations where money is discussed, because they'll have a base of knowledge to ground them.

We're not talking financial literacy on the expert level; your kids don't need to know the equation to predict the future value of a dollar. But, do they know who to call for help with their taxes? That's good. Do they seek out financial advice proactively before making major financial decisions, like buying a house or investing in a business? Even better. Do they know *who* to ask for help? Do they know *when*? Do they know *what* questions? That's ideal. If your kids have that kind of familiarity with financial literacy and a circle of expert guides, they will be significantly insulated against the kind of negative influence that might come from a spouse. Again, you can refer to our Appendix for suggestions on how to form a team of these experts.

Youth sports have helped us experience how competence breeds confidence. When our kids started hockey, they couldn't skate. Fear and anxiety nearly prevented them from ever getting on the ice. But by patiently coaching them through the tears, we were able to help them develop fundamental skills that gave them the confidence to move on and enhance their skills. Financial literacy can work the same way.

With great wealth comes a greater need for depth of knowledge. We want to raise our kids to be family stewards, which means they need to be prepared to take financial leadership in their families. We want them to ask the right questions, so they can get the right answers.

How do we get there? If we want our kids to internalize the Family Vision and our family values, we start by *showing* them good financial habits, *sharing* lessons and stories of family, and *surrounding* them with good influences. Then, we work to create a foundation of financial literacy for them to build on in the future.

Luckily, that is exactly what our next chapter is all about.

PART TWO

FINANCIAL LITERACY

*Pass on financial literacy fundamentals to
your children and grandchildren through
experiences, lessons, and by strengthening your
own understanding of financial concepts.*

CHAPTER THREE

FINANCIAL EXPERIENCES

"Tell me and I forget. Teach me and I remember. Involve me and I learn."

BEN FRANKLIN

Anna and Will like to bake. Anything sweet will do, though brownies and cupcakes usually top the list of their culinary priorities. Both of us have to brace ourselves when our children threaten to take over the kitchen—mainly because both of us enjoy things being *clean*.

We all know what happens when small children grab the mixing bowl and eggs. The eggshells fall into the bowl, and each small piece needs to be fished out. The kids need to be schlepped over to the sink to wash their hands again, only to have the experience repeated with the second egg—and let's not even talk about what happens with the flour. A process that we could have accomplished in twenty minutes ends up taking close to an hour.

Yet, we do it. We allow the kids to roll up their sleeves and ransack the pantry. Why?

We like that they feel a sense of accomplishment at the end of it all. We like seeing them learn the importance of following detailed instructions carefully—like, the order really *does* matter, and sometimes you really *do* have to blend it instead of whisking it. We like seeing them become competent in new skills. Plus, we like eating their brownies.

Giving your children financial experiences often involves similar messiness and hassles. However, the rewards that come from their growing financial literacy are profound—even more so than gooey chocolate desserts, fresh out of the oven.

In our previous chapter, we talked about *teaching* your kids important financial values through modeling smart financial behaviors. Your instruction will help them remember the financial behaviors and values they observed from you, and it's certain those memories will inform their actions down the road.

However, to witness true financial *learning* in your children—regardless of their age—we believe, it's necessary to *involve* them in financial experiences. Would it be easier for you to manage their money all the way through college graduation? Yes. That would likely involve far less mess. But, just as we want to raise kids who can cook for themselves as adults, we also want to raise kids who are financially literate—and we're guessing our readers do too.

We want to take a moment to clarify the difference between financial *education* and financial *literacy*. **Financial education is the formal instruction on formulas and concepts. Financial literacy is the ability to *apply* financial knowledge and, in our opinion, includes the motivation, confidence, and experience to manage wealth responsibly.** In order for your kids to develop this ability to *apply* their financial knowledge, they need practice. That's what this chapter is all about.

Financial literacy is one of the most profound gifts you can give to your children and grandchildren, and it's never too late to begin. In this chapter, we've compiled a number of financial experiences that will enable your kids to get involved with money management, and we've tried to suggest ways you could translate the concepts at various ages. For simplicity's sake, we're going to discuss these illustrations as you could do them with "your children," but these financial experiences could also be carried out with grandparents and grandchildren, or aunts and uncles with nieces and nephews. There are also specific suggestions for how each activity can scale up from "kids" to full grown adults. We encourage you to take these ideas and run with them, in the way that will best suit your family, your context, and your needs.

In the chapters that follow, we'll also cover some foundational concepts to strengthen the financial *education* pieces. Ideally, your young people will get a mixture of both financial education and literacy, so they can handle their finances with both knowledge *and* wisdom.

MONEY MANAGEMENT: ROGER NARRATES

I vividly remember the season of life when my high-school football team started lifting weights. My coach had each player set long- and short-term goals for the different power lifts. Training with weights made it easy to set goals that were specific and measurable, but keeping kids motivated and committed was the coaches' real challenge.

To meet that challenge, the coaches regularly reminded us of our *purpose* with building up strength: they emphasized that all our effort went toward helping us prevent injuries, protect our teammates and friends, improve our performance, and compete at a higher level. Our shared purpose was our high-school football team's version of a Family Vision. Ultimately, our workouts started to feel characterized by the idea that our individual efforts were all building up a stronger team.

Our coaches also set up a system of accountability. Everyone had a written program that provided us with direction in the gym and helped us log progress. At the end of each month, the team gathered in the powerlifting room where one station for each powerlift was set up. One by one, each of my teammates stepped up and took a shot at beating their previous max lift for each of the powerlifts. It was inspiring.

Now: why would a section on money management start off with a discussion about power lifts and football players? In our opinion, the key to effective money management all ties into goal-setting—and this was the best experience I've had with learning how to set and achieve goals. The other players and I had short-term goals of increasing our personal bests every month, along with the long-term goal of strengthening our abilities as a unified team. Similarly, **smart family stewards learn how to juggle short-term spending needs with long-term financial goals.**

In this section, we're *not* going to tell you how to teach your kids to format a budgeting spreadsheet. As financial advisors, we have found that attempts to adhere to a strict budget can often be exhausting, complicated, and ultimately unproductive. On the other hand, our most successful clients manage their money effectively by keeping different financial goals in mind. That's what we want to recommend you teach your kids: the juggling act of meeting short-term needs, while pursuing long-term financial goals.

Goals-based money management could be thought of as "bucketizing." The idea behind bucketizing is that you're separating your money into different "buckets," (i.e., assets), according to what you want to do with that money, and when. For instance, you might have a checking account bucket, which has money for all your immediate spending needs. You might have a savings account bucket for emergency funds. You might have a retirement bucket, possibly a college savings account bucket, and a world cruise bucket as well. Each bucket has a different purpose and a different time horizon; therefore, it's fitting to use different investment strategies for each one.

These different buckets are all ways to manage your money which are based on *goals*. Your retirement bucket has the goal of providing a living for you after you retire; given that goal, you're not going to use *that* money to buy your next Starbucks latte. You're going to let it sit, grow, contribute to it, and access it decades after you started it. Through helping your kids identify different buckets for short-term, intermediate, and long-term financial goals, you can help them see more clearly how their money should be dispensed or saved. The alternative, which is spending money from one big bucket, can make people more vulnerable to impulse buying.

It's important to note that goals-based money management is not a universally recommended practice. When looked at through the lens of financial theory, one could argue that goals-based money management could create inefficiencies on potential investment results. To break that down, once you start separating your money and opening new accounts, your overall investment portfolio will look different than it would if all your money were lumped together.

However, in our opinion, the pros of goals-based money management outweigh the cons. We like how "bucketizing" drives behavior. It prompts people to identify their financial goals and aids in managing expectations.

With all that in mind, our set of activities listed to teach money management focuses on how you can teach the concepts of goals-based money management and determining financial priorities.

MONEY MANAGEMENT WITH KIDS

Let's talk **allowance**. Many families like to associate allowances with doing chores, which is a legitimate strategy. It's teaching kids that they earn money through hard work. However, the two of us have decided to make allowances separate from doing work. We explain to our kids that they should view their allowance as a tool to learn how to manage money. In essence: the allowance *is* the work.

Here's one way to do it, which gives kids a nice visual of bucketizing their money. Come allowance time, we set up a series of Mason jars on our kitchen counter. Jack will start earning an allowance when he's five; for now, the dollars are meted out just to Will and Anna. Each month Anna and Will receive as many dollars as they are years old. As of this writing, Will gets $7.00, and Anna gets $9.00.

The jars have signs on them: "Big Savings: 50%," "Little Savings: 40%," and "Help Others: 10%." The kids deposit their money in the jars, according to the percentages. We take the money from the "Big Savings" jar, and invest it in the Family Bank—more on that in just a minute.

The "Little Savings" jar is their spending money, but by calling it "Little Savings," we're trying to reinforce the idea that you don't just run out with that money and blow it all on gumballs. That's the money that Will saves for his next Bucks t-shirt. They can choose to buy candy with it too, of course, but there are other spending priorities associated with their "Little Savings" money as well. The money in the "Help Others" jar is what they take to church every Sunday and drop in the offering basket and they also use to save up for a year-end donation to a special charity of choice.

In giving our kids the visual of these jars, we're hoping to teach them several key principles. One, we want them to learn to live beneath their means; that's why their "Little Savings/Spending" percentage is *smaller* than the percentage devoted to the "Big Savings" jar.

Secondly, we try to give them a long view of their money's purpose through discussing the goals of the "Big Savings" money. There's that goal-setting element: we identify goals far into the future to help them appreciate the value of delayed gratification with their money. We tailor the "Big Savings" discussion to our kids' maturity level. Although Anna might be able to envision wanting to buy a car some-day, Will needs a "Big Savings" goal that feels a little more immediately rewarding—maybe something like a big bas-ketball hoop or a dirt bike.

Finally, we want to reinforce the value of giving to others. By building up a habit of setting aside 10 percent of every-thing they make for charity, we're hoping to ingrain giving as a lifestyle habit. We want them to remember that they are blessed, and they therefore have a responsibility to give to others as well.

WITH TEENAGERS

Once your kids are older, you can give them more respon-sibility with managing their money. Here are a few ideas:

- **Put your child in charge of the Target run, or the grocery trip.** Teach them to compare unit prices among items, and give them a finite amount of money to cover everything on the list. You can also do this with their own personal expenses: give them a certain amount of money for their back-to-school clothes and supplies. They might be especially motivated in those cases to learn how to get the most bang for their buck!
- Take this same concept, and expand your kids' respon-sibilities. **Put your child in charge of managing your**

family's budget for a weekend or during a trip. Help them identify what the biggest expenses will be, and where they might need to get creative about making the money stretch. You can help them monitor expenses in a number of ways—teach them about balancing a check book; show them how to monitor an account balance online; or, even give them an envelope with cash that needs to cover all expenses for the experience they're leading.

- **Teach your kids and grandkids the "bucketizing" process.** When Roger was younger, his mom encouraged him to "bucketize" by putting a certain amount of his money toward regular expenses, like car insurance and gas, save money for less frequent expenses, like buying new clothes, and save toward the long-term goal of buying his first computer. As a college student, his practice in "bucketizing" enabled him to juggle his various expenses with housing, books, student fees, and food.

- Rather than covering expenses for your kids outright, like their cell phone bill or car insurance, **have them go in on bills with you.** This helps cure kids of the expectation that everything will be handed to them, and will make them more thoughtful about how they handle their money. When kids have a vested interest in their expenses, they're more motivated to think critically about their cell phone plan, for instance, or ways to bring their insurance costs down.

- Some of our wealthiest clients have urged their kids to get **high-school jobs.** Although these parents could provide for every desire these kids could invent, the parents want their children to understand what it means to work and save for their own spending money. They also think it's valuable for kids to realize how much is taken out in taxes.

- Once kids are in college, you may decide you want to provide them with spending money. If so, **make them give you a budgeting statement** which shows how they spent it. We have a friend who had his daughter complete this every month. She had to put together an Excel spreadsheet, identify categories of expenses, and specifically note what she spent her money on. At the end of one month, she complained to her dad about her stressful finals load and begged to skip the budget report. He told her no! "That's not how the world works," he said. "Your creditors won't give you a pass just because you're stressed out. If you owe the money, you need to pay the money when it's due, regardless of what else is going on in your life." We think this is a clever strategy — even if it does require some tough love!

WITH ADULT CHILDREN

By the time your children have grown into adults, they'll already have a number of financial habits ingrained. The impressions they got about money as kids will be their default assumptions as they handle finances. Still, that doesn't mean they can't learn new concepts of financial literacy, or develop a deeper appreciation for your family's financial vision. Here are some suggestions for bringing your adult children into financial educational experiences:

- **If and when you gift money to your adult children, have a conversation about your expectations for how they'll use it.** Use these gifts as an opportunity for conversation and education. Let them know if the money is meant to be invested for their retirement, or in another long-term financial asset, like a 529 college savings plan for your grandchildren. If you want to see them enjoy the funds on extracurricular activities, then tell them that. If this is a gifting strategy you only plan on doing for a particular time period and not indefinitely, tell them that so everyone knows what to expect. When there's no conversation, both the giver and the receiver may be disappointed in the outcome of how the gift is used.

- **Help your children and grandchildren plan for the future by bringing financial conversations back to the concept of long-term goals.** You can do this by identifying your own savings priorities reflected in your different asset "buckets." We work with clients who put aside money in one bucket to give to their kids as an inheritance, but they still encourage their kids to save and invest money in their own buckets so that they're learning to be financially independent. For example, you might guide your children or grandchildren to put six to twelve months of emergency funds in readily accessible accounts; savings for a new car in an appropriate short-term investment vehicle; and savings for retirement in a long-term investment vehicle.

- **Bring them to meetings with members of your financial team.** It can be especially valuable for grown children to have these meetings when they're going over their first job package, for instance, or looking to set up their first 401(k). Financial advisors can help educate them about different financial strategies that they may not yet have been exposed to, and can help walk them through seminal financial experiences, like buying a house for the first time. Your kids will also feel less intimidated about seeking out financial experts if they're exposed to the experience of meeting with a financial advisor early on. See our Appendix for recommendations on how to assemble this team.

- As your children continue to age, **increase their involvement in your family's estate management.** Do as much as you can to expose them to your financial priorities and give them opportunities to work alongside you in managing your estate. Ideally, by the time you're ready to give over that power completely, you will have full confidence in your children to continue the good work in your absence.

THE FAMILY BANK

Around the time we set up our kids' allowance Mason jars, we had to talk about what we were going to do with the money that went into the "Big Savings" jar. We agreed that, given our kids' young ages, we would invest the money for them. But how?

When we started the process with Anna at age five, we felt she was too young to have her own savings account in a bank—and, to be honest, we didn't want to bother driving her to the bank to make a formal deposit every time she got her allowance! Besides, we mused, the interest rates on savings accounts were so low, we weren't confident she would be able to recognize the value of leaving her few dollars in the bank.

Thus, our version of **The Family Bank** was born, which is mainly characterized by an Excel worksheet, and spectacular interest rates. Here's how it works:

When Anna and Will put their money in the "Big Savings"

jar, we "deposit" their money into our Family Bank, which basically means they hand the money back to Roger. We calculate their new balance and give them a balance receipt via an Excel spreadsheet. In order to help our kids recognize that money in a savings account earns interest, we pay them 10 percent annual interest. Admittedly, that's far above current market rates, but it's big enough that the kids take notice—especially when they see the effect of compounding interest.

Because Anna is able to see how noticeably her account is growing in the Family Bank, she is able to weigh that investment over the temptation of an impulse buy. On a recent Target trip, when we asked her if she *really* wanted to buy those unicorn socks, she thought about it and then said, "Nah. I think I'll leave my money in the Family Bank instead." Success!

When our kids want to buy a big-ticket item, we walk them through making a withdrawal. We calculate their new balance, give them a receipt, and then give them the cash they've "withdrawn." On a practical level, the actual cash is either deposited or withdrawn from our own wallets or bank accounts. We simply keep track of the money for them, and grow it, through our Excel spreadsheet calculations.

The best part of this strategy—we're having regular dialogues with our kids about their money. Finances are a comfortable and open topic. We've had countless opportunities to grow their financial literacy and get a sense of their financial habits. They're engaging with us in a transparent way about their financial priorities, and we're learning about their level of responsibility.

THE FAMILY BANK FOR TEENS AND ADULTS

The Family Bank concept is easy to scale up. Anytime parents give their children loans, they're using the same concept of the Family Bank. Using their own capital, the parents are able to give their children more advantageous rates than if their children were getting loans. Here's how this might work:

- Provide a loan to your grown children from the Family Bank for a "big ticket" item, with better interest rates than a bank loan. If your child wants to buy a car, or needs help with a down payment for their first house, it's a common time for parents to give financial help to their kids. Do yourself and your child a favor, and formalize this agreement. By writing out terms and a contract, you not only help educate your child about the way the loans work, you also create some healthy boundaries and clear expectations. Those terms will provide accountability to your child and encourage them to be responsible, while also giving them healthy "real-world" practice in meeting regular loan payments. However, by giving them an improved interest rate over a bank, you're still providing generous help.
- Provide a business loan to your children. Parents with enough liquid capital may have the resources to give their children a large loan direct from their own Family Bank. You have the opportunity to dialogue with your child about money. Your partnership with them also opens the door to talk about other financially-related issues that would normally be taboo—like, "Are you paying your bills? What is your salary?" If your children want your financial help, offer it to them in dollar bills *and* education.

INVESTING EXPERIENCES

One of our family traditions involves a summer road trip to Maine where we enjoy time at our family cabin. Between Wisconsin and Maine the lunch stop choices are pretty much McDonald's, Starbucks, and sometimes a pizza place.

On one stop at McDonald's, Roger told our two oldest, "You know, you could own a piece of this company."

"What? How?" Will asked. "Are you going to buy a McDonald's?!" Our recent real estate ventures had given Anna and Will newfound zeal for buying property! But Roger corrected them. He explained that what he was talking about was owning *stock* in McDonald's.

This was a big new concept for them, and the topic of conversation for the rest of that McDonald's visit. Both Anna and Will could easily come up with ten investible companies that they like: Under Armour, Nike, McDonald's, and so on. Every so often, we try to get them to consider what it might be like to own shares in those companies. At a young age, we're only *talking* to our kids about stock investments; the goal, at this point, is simply to plant seeds.

As a summer project, in the future we might help them track the McDonald's stock, to think about how a company's share price might fluctuate. Once they're a little older, we'll actually buy them some shares of a stock they like. We've already done this for our nieces and nephews. We purchased stock in one of their favorite companies, made up a certificate of ownership for them, and gave it to them for their high school graduation so they had a tangible proof of their investment.

When our niece and nephew asked us how their stocks would work, we explained the share price would change and probably grow, so they'd want to monitor it over time. We explained that the stock we'd bought them would produce dividends, which meant they would have the option to receive money from those dividends every quarter, or they could choose to use those dividends to buy more shares. It was a basic explanation, but for both of them, it was an eye-opening introduction to stock investments—and that was the goal. The size of the gift was not life changing, but it was an effective way to teach and influence behavior.

WITH TEENS AND ADULT CHILDREN

The older the kid, the more they can begin to understand about investing. Here are some ideas about how you can take this concept further:

- **Help young adults track stocks in a variety of investment categories.** Work with them to prepare a model portfolio and track their progress. You can find information about a stock's performance in a number of places—the newspaper, online, and even via some apps. Show them the S&P 500 versus the movement of an individual stock, and discuss the pros and cons. Consider whether or not it might be appropriate to help them purchase some of those stocks.
- **If a teen or young adult inherits money, help them invest it.** Granted, it can be fun and educational for kids to track their favorite companies by watching individual stocks. However, it may be most prudent financially for a first investment to go into an index fund, like the S&P 500. An index fund investment will be simpler to track

for your child, and will also provide immediate diversification across a variety of companies and sectors, which helps lower risk. (Individual stocks can be more volatile in their performance, as we'll discuss in chapter five.)

- **Set up a meeting for your adult child with your trusted financial advisor.** Again, this early exposure to investment advising and financial planning will help your children take the next step in becoming financially literate. Your children will begin to wrap their heads around investment concepts and strategies as well as build a foundation for a sound financial plan.

GIVING

Raising our kids with the value of giving is obviously important to us—we've already brought it up with the Mason jars, and in the Family Vision. We think giving back is key to experiencing fulfillment and meaning in life, and our clients who practice giving seem to attest to this. Here's one strategy we're going to implement with our own kids in the next year.

Throughout the year, we give to charities that are near and dear to our hearts. We also volunteer our time and give to our church. While our children have been at such young ages, we felt like it was enough to simply model our family value of giving; their observation of our efforts was their way of participating. Now that the kids are older, we want to actually get them involved in the experience. This year, we're going to include our kids in a conversation about what charities to give to—both to discuss *our* giving and where they may want to gift *their* 10 percent from the "Helping Others" jar.

Given that Will and Anna are both still pretty young, we'll likely put together a short list of charities that are local or that have gotten top rankings on either GuideStar or Charity Navigator.[21] We'll put together options that we know would appeal to them. For instance, Anna may be interested in supporting Wisconsin Literacy because of her love of reading. Will may want to support a hockey-themed charity called Inner City Education (ICE) because of his love for hockey. Then we'll ask them about what other ideas they might have, and if they can think of other organizations they'd want to give to.

As they get even older, we'll push them to research charities on their own. We'll ask them to look into the charity's budget: how much money actually goes to the program? How much goes to staff? How much goes to advertising? Is there a certain arm of this charity that you want to specify your money going to? Do they have a history of being financially responsible, or overreaching themselves?

Roy Williams and Vic Preisser, authors of *Preparing Heirs*, note that sharing experiences of philanthropy together as a family can be valuable as a learning experience, but also hugely important in carrying on a Family Vision. In discussing opportunities to participate in family philanthropy, the authors write: "These opportunities are often unifying and personally fulfilling for the heirs, and are opportunities to learn and test family values. Equally important, philanthropic decision-making involvement begins to teach the heirs early lessons about decisions, money, and accountability."[22]

---

21 Guidestar and Charity Navigator are both reputable organizations which rate not-for-profit organizations.

22 Williams, Roy O., and Vic Preisser. *Preparing Heirs: Five Steps to a Successful Transition of Family Wealth and Values.* Bandon: Robert D. Reed Publishers, 2015.

In other words, participating in philanthropy can help kids internalize your Family Vision—moving it from words on a paper to a heartfelt personal value. It can also open their eyes to the importance of some of the practical economics that make the world run, like ensuring a non-profit is using their money well.

Giving of time and talent can be just as rewarding and important. When possible, encourage your kids to volunteer for the charities they're especially excited about. You can start the process by including them in your own volunteerism, and eventually empower them to seek out their own volunteer opportunities. For example, over the past fourteen years our business has sponsored a breast cancer fundraiser; for the last three years, Anna has helped Lori volunteer at the actual event. In those three years, Anna has witnessed hundreds of runners passing by with ribbons marked, "In Memory Of", "In Honor Of", and "Survivor." In other words, she recognizes why everyone is there that day. In the first couple years, her volunteerism was prompted by our urging, but this past year, *she* asked *us* if she could volunteer again. That was a proud parenting moment!

Your children or grandchildren might feel especially excited if the same organization gets both their money and time. For example, if they're mentoring kids through Big Brothers/ Big Sisters, they'll feel that much more personal investment in the charity. They'll also experience more immediacy in their act of giving by getting to know the people who benefit from their gifts, firsthand. As an added bonus, they'll become better acquainted with the strengths and weaknesses of how a non-profit is run.

Many kids grow up to be on the boards of non-profits. Some kids will eventually run their family's charitable foundation. Consider the benefits you might be able to provide these philanthropic adults if you start building their knowledge base early on. These future leaders will have a much better understanding of what it means to do due diligence, and they'll be thoughtful about how to best make an impact on society.

OTHER ACTIVITIES

Several other experiences can help your kids internalize the values that will lead to becoming great family stewards. The experiences below can help them develop diligence, delayed gratification, and goal-setting—all of which will help them become successful, financially savvy adults.

- Give your kids **rewards for their diligence.** The book *Thou Shall Prosper*, by Rabbi Daniel Lapin, gives a fascinating picture of what this looks like in a Jewish community.[23] At Hanukah, children are given money that reflects their success, their level of education, their performance in Hebrew classes, and so on. The tradition reinforces the principle that, "You win if you achieve." Children who receive these rewards learn that educating oneself is the best way to increase one's potential. You can adapt this strategy by identifying the values that you want to reinforce in your kids, and make a big deal over them when you see them living out those values. Compliment them when you see good manners, kind gestures, empathy, or support—or give them tangible

23 Lapin, Daniel. *Thou Shall Prosper: Ten Commandments for Making Money.* Hoboken, NJ: John Wiley & Sons, 2010.

rewards. You might say, "Since everyone was so helpful today, we can go to the park." In doing so, you'll communicate the message that their good choices will lead to good things.

- You can help teach your kids **delayed gratification** by offering delayed rewards. We've already discussed the "Wait two weeks" line from Lori's grandfather, but it's even more valuable for your kids to live out experiences where gratification comes after waiting. Here's one idea: after your children have saved a certain amount of money, reward them by allowing them to purchase something that they've been wanting for a while. Or, after they have read so many books off their shelf, you will buy them a new one. Regular experiences of working, waiting, and *then* receiving rewards will help your kids learn the invaluable skill of practicing delayed gratification.

- Incorporate **goal-setting** throughout the areas of your life. If you're looking for a place to begin, you could try January 1! Every New Years, we sit down and write some goals for the year—usually short term and long term. Anna's past goals have included new athletic moves she wants to learn in gymnastics and ice-skating; Will's goal was to save up enough to get a dirt bike. Lori's goal was to be on a women's hockey team by age forty, and Roger's goal was to learn to play the ukulele. At the beginning of each new school quarter, you could set academic goals; at the start of new sports seasons, you could identify athletic goals. Help your kids (and yourself) take action on those goals by committing to a class, or a new routine. Once the goals are identified, do what you can to empower your kids to achieve them— and don't forget the importance of following through on your own! Seeing Mom and Dad (or Grandpa and Grandma!) learning new things at "old" ages shows them that we can be lifetime learners.

"INVOLVE ME AND I LEARN"

Financially responsible kids turn into financially responsible adults—and financially *irresponsible* kids may turn into finally *irresponsible* adults, if they're not given opportunities to learn how to handle their money well. If we want our kids to learn how to cook, we have to let them get dirty in the kitchen. If we want true learning in the area of financial literacy, kids have to try these experiences out themselves.

By guiding your children into financial experiences when they're still impressionable, you can actively help your kids develop the financial values you want them to practice as adults. Shape your conversations around what results, and take it to the next level of depth when you sense that they're ready.

What do we mean when we say "next level of depth"? That's exactly where we're going next.

CHAPTER FOUR

FINANCIAL LITERACY FUNDAMENTALS

*"In economics, one of the most important concepts is oppor-
tunity cost—the idea that once you spend your money on
something, you can't spend it again on something else."*

MALCOLM TURNBULL

Our daughter Anna is enrolled in gymnastics. It's been fun
to see her graduate from doing a clumsy somersault, to a
confident cartwheel, to a perfectly executed roundoff-back-
handspring. The two of us had a good laugh the other day,
though, when we imagined what it would look like if either
of us attempted to start learning gymnastics. We would
probably break our necks!

In essence, Anna is experiencing, in bodily form, the effects
of compound interest. Stay with us for a second. Let's say
Anna's *present value* is her current strength and flexibility.
That's what she's got to work with, today. As she *invests*
her time and effort through working out, building muscle,
and increasing her flexibility, she's able to develop these

new skills with exponential speed. As she gets older, all of her skills and physical fitness will continue to build on each another, and she's going to keep getting better. That's very similar to how your money can build on itself when you invest young and give it the benefit of time.

Now, let's return to the middle-aged parents watching from the sidelines, laughing about what it would look like if we attempted a back handspring. If we were absolutely determined to develop some skills in gymnastics, we might be able to make it happen with a lot of time in the gym and a lot of hard work. Even then, there's no way we'd ever be able to catch up with the skill of our third grader, and her flexible, strong, little body. Time is simply not on our side! Similarly, it's much harder, and takes much longer, to build up your wealth if you start later in life. The power of compound interest is mainly rooted in time.

Although the two of us missed out on our opportunity for back handsprings, Anna's coaches didn't. Some of them are in their fifties and even sixties, but they can do the moves they teach the kids. They started young and have decades' worth of muscle memory. Their years of investment mean that they are now reaping the benefits. They are incredibly flexible, strong, and can do amazing things with their bodies—which we, who are younger than they are, could never do. They, too, are experiencing the benefits of compound interest.

In this chapter, we turn our attention to financial literacy and provide you with some tools to teach your kids and grandkids financial lessons (like the one about compound interest). Don't worry; we'll discuss that more in a second, with more numbers and less metaphor. In some cases, we'll include activities you can use to help teach financial concepts. However, we're now getting into some of the more involved financial concepts, and many of the concepts won't easily lend themselves to an activity. Some of them simply need to be explained or taught.

Our goal with this chapter is to clearly explain some foundational concepts with the objective of building financial literacy. You may already understand many of these ideas, but perhaps you don't have the simple language you might need to break it down for your kids. Or, maybe you already know many of these concepts, but you would prefer to have your teenagers or adult children read these chapters on their own. Some of our readers may feel fuzzy on these concepts and would appreciate a refresher.

Why are these concepts important? Each generation needs to have basic concepts of financial literacy in order to stay on course with making informed decisions. We're going to start this chapter with some big picture aspects of financial literacy, and we'll delve into more specific areas of finance in Chapter Five.

As you review our explanations and advice, you may recognize ways you can help your kids connect the dots between these concepts and what gets them excited—just like Anna's gymnastics turned into a great opportunity to talk about compound interest.

COMPOUND INTEREST

Let's begin by more fully unpacking Anna's back handspring and what it can teach us about compound interest. Einstein once called the power of compound interest the most powerful force in the universe. Reportedly, he said, "Compound interest is the eighth wonder of the world. He who understands it, earns it...He who doesn't... pays it."[24]

Here's how it works: when your money is earning interest, time becomes a major factor. The longer you give your money to build, the more your money actually works for you. When you track interest graphically, the curve becomes exponential as interest is gained on the principal and previous accumulated interest.

Let's take an example of two people, Mary and Bill, who both decide they want to start putting aside money for retirement. Mary gets a jump on this project early, starting at age twenty-four. She invests $10,000 a year for ten years, putting $100,000 total in her retirement account.

Bill puts his retirement goals off an additional decade, and starts putting aside money at age thirty-four. He also invests $10,000 a year and continues to invest until he retires, ultimately putting in $320,000. Here's a picture of their two exponential curves, based on their different starting points[25]:

---

24 Cannivet, Michael. "How Einstein Would Manage His
     Portfolio." Forbes. Forbes Magazine, December 7, 2017.
     https://www.forbes.com/sites/michaelcannivet/2017/12/07/
     how-einstein-would-manage-his-portfolio/#5bf4636a12b2.

25 NOTE: Chart assumes contributions are made at the beginning of the year and at
     an 8 percent annual rate of return. It is for illustrative purposes only and is not a
     guarantee of future interest rates or financial returns.

THE IMPACT OF SAVING EARLY

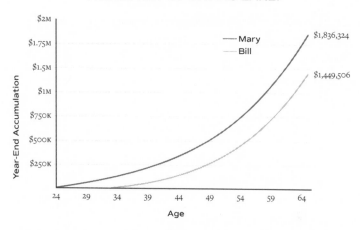

Obviously, Mary's curve ended up much higher than Bill's — approaching $400,000 higher — even though she only put in $100,000 compared to his investment of $320,000. Why would that be?

The answer: time. Mary gave herself an additional ten years to let that interest compound, and it was in those final ten years that her curve shot up at its steepest. Let's take a closer look at how those numbers work.

THE IMPACT OF SAVING EARLY

	MARY			BILL	
Age	Deposit	Year-End Accumulation	Age	Deposit	Year-End Accumulation
24	$10,000	$10,800	24	—	—
25	$10,000	$22,464	25	—	—
26	$10,000	$35,061	26	—	—
27	$10,000	$48,666	27	—	—
28	$10,000	$63,359	28	—	—
29	$10,000	$79,228	29	—	—
30	$10,000	$96,366	30	—	—
31	$10,000	$114,876	31	—	—
32	$10,000	$134,866	32	—	—
33	$10,000	$156,455	33	—	—
34	—	$168,971	34	$10,000	$10,800
35	—	$182,489	35	$10,000	$22,464
36	—	$197,088	36	$10,000	$35,061
37	—	$212,855	37	$10,000	$48,666
38	—	$229,884	38	$10,000	$63,359
39	—	$248,274	39	$10,000	$79,228
40	—	$268,136	40	$10,000	$96,366
41	—	$289,587	41	$10,000	$114,876
42	—	$312,754	42	$10,000	$134,866
43	—	$337,774	43	$10,000	$156,455
44	—	$364,796	44	$10,000	$179,771
45	—	$393,980	45	$10,000	$204,953
46	—	$425,498	46	$10,000	$232,149
47	—	$459,538	47	$10,000	$261,521
48	—	$496,301	48	$10,000	$293,243
49	—	$536,005	49	$10,000	$327,502
50	—	$578,886	50	$10,000	$364,502
51	—	$625,197	51	$10,000	$404,463
52	—	$675,212	52	$10,000	$447,620
53	—	$729,229	53	$10,000	$494,229
54	—	$787,568	54	$10,000	$544,568
55	—	$850,573	55	$10,000	$598,933
56	—	$918,619	56	$10,000	$657,648

57	—	$992,109	57	$10,000	$721,059
58	—	$1,071,477	58	$10,000	$789,544
59	—	$1,157,196	59	$10,000	$863,508
60	—	$1,249,771	60	$10,000	$943,388
61	—	$1,349,753	61	$10,000	$1,029,832
62	—	$1,457,733	62	$10,000	$1,122,832
63	—	$1,574,352	63	$10,000	$1,223,459
64	—	$1,700,300	64	$10,000	$1,332,135
65	—	$1,836,324	65	$10,000	$1,449,506
Total	$100,000		Total	$320,000	

These two graphics spell out the power of compound interest: Bill's extra investment of $220,000 couldn't compete with Mary's extra *time*. Just like Anna's efforts in gymnastics, starting young makes a huge difference. The power of time can make your money grow exponentially.

The formula for compound interest is very simple: the power of compound interest comes from raising the time variable to the exponential power.

The future value of an investment = the present value$(1 +$ the interest rate$)^n$

Much of the power, strength, and growth of compound interest comes from "the nth degree": time. This is why we believe in the power of saving early: to be able to achieve exponential growth.

Once you have accomplished a successful principal investment that will benefit from years of building compound interest, you have done a lot of the heavy lifting for the next generation. The next generation will begin with a larger number already in place to compound again for the next generation beyond that. If the "nth" degree ends up representing multiple generations, an investment has the ability to gain momentum, growing powerfully and *sustaining* multiple generations. However, for that growth to be maintained, future generations need to understand the power at work in their accounts. That's why each new generation needs a basic understanding of compound interest.

It's a common investing mistake to solely focus on the interest rate or rate of return. In reality, this is not the most powerful component in the equation; the most powerful component is time. The longer you wait to start saving, the more strapped you'll be in the future.

Consider, again, the example of Mary and Bill. Bill may have thought to himself, "I'm not going to worry about saving for retirement in my twenties. I have plenty of time to worry about that, and I'm not making much money right now anyway." However, as it worked out for Bill, he had to start his savings efforts at age thirty-four. What are people doing at age thirty-four? For many, that's a stage of life with already high expenses, like a mortgage or kids' activities. What's more, because Bill started investing later, he had to keep investing every year, for thirty years—ultimately paying $320,000 out-of-pocket.

Mary may not have been making much as a twenty-four-year-old—but she decided she'd rather save money for her retirement early so that she could invest in other things later on. Maybe she opted for a less desirable apartment to get her $10,000 logged away, or perhaps she ate out less often. As a result, she was able to let her money work for her. She stopped investing in her retirement after ten years, yet she still ended up with more than Bill. By making those sacrifices in her twenties, Mary was freed up in her thirties and forties to invest money in a better house, in her family, and in any number of other financial goals. She got her money in early and let it do the hard work for her.

As powerful as compound interest can be in building wealth, its exponential momentum can also work against you. Compound interest can make debt a real challenge to overcome, especially if both your debt and your interest are large. We'll talk more about this in our next chapter.

WHAT IT MEANS TO BE FINANCIALLY INDEPENDENT

Our next topic is a big one: what it means to be financially independent. Elsewhere in this book, we've talked about a misperception that can sometimes affect wealthy people—the idea that the money will always last.

If we were to sit down with those people, we might be able to work out whether or not their lifestyle is *draining* their estate, or is actually being supported by the growth from their assets. That's an important question: if you want your children and grandchildren to "pass it on," they need to be maintaining their wealth (at least). Ideally, they would be building it.

This is personal for us. By living within our means and investing for financial security, we will likely leave our kids an inheritance. We want to make sure our kids grow into financially responsible adults and perpetuate any wealth they receive. In order to do that, we need to teach them what it means to be financially independent.

Some people assume that financial independence simply means you have a job and you can pay your bills. However, that's not true independence. **To be financially independent means you have the ability to live off the income and growth of your investments, along with any fixed income sources; you are not reliant on an employer for a paycheck.** In other words, work becomes optional. You don't *have* to work to meet your expenses, so you're therefore independent. If you've got multiple sources of income, diversified assets, and multiple categories of expenses, this question of financial independence can be tricky to answer.

Our experience is that most people strive to achieve financial independence. You may come across some general rules of thumb for determining independence:

- Portfolio value ÷ monthly expenses = months of available income
- Annual expense ÷ portfolio value = (should ideally equal) 3 to 4 percent

If you'd like to consider the question of financial independence using the notion of goal-based investing and mental accounting, we're about to illustrate it more fully with the diagrams that follow. At first glance, the diagrams look complex, but we're going to break it down, one piece at a time. This is not intended to be a full financial plan but a "back of the napkin" starting point. The question of *your* financial independence would be best discussed, in all its particular detail, with a financial advisor.

EVALUATING FINANCIAL INDEPENDENCE

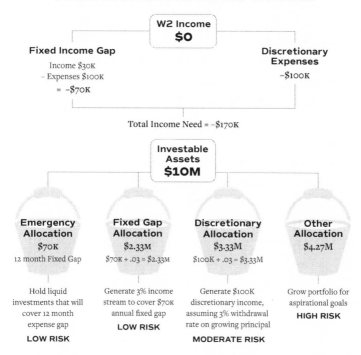

The diagram has two levels, and we're going to take them one at a time. Let's look at the top level first, which helps establish your income needs.

ESTIMATING INCOME NEED

On the top level of this chart is a box labeled "W-2 Income." That box represents the money earned from a paycheck. Two branches come off of that box: the one coming off the left is labeled "Fixed Income Gap;" the one coming off the right is labeled "Discretionary Expenses." Let's focus on the fixed income gap concept first.

What we're looking to understand through determining the fixed income gap is the gap (or difference) between what you earn through your fixed income versus what you spend through your fixed expenses. Fixed income is the money you receive every year, reliably, on a regular schedule. A good example would be Social Security or pension income. Similarly, fixed expenses are also required, reliably, on a regular schedule, such as a mortgage payment, a business loan payment, insurance payments, the cost of groceries, utility bills, and so on.

Let's say we're dealing with a retiree named Joe. Because Joe isn't working anymore, he doesn't have any W-2 income. In the top "W-2 Income" circle, then, Joe would write "zero." However, Joe still has some fixed income, coming to him via a pension and social security; it totals $30,000 per year. Note that Joe also has about $100,000 in fixed expenses. His fixed gap is his fixed income ($30,000) minus his fixed expenses ($100,000), which equals *negative* $70,000.

Got it so far? If you're tracking, you know that Joe is going to have to figure out a way to cover his net gap of -$70,000 if he wants to eat and keep his lights on. For the sake of the example, we're keeping this simple and not including taxes or inflation into this equation at this time.

Now let's look at the discretionary arm, labeled "Discretionary Expenses." Discretionary expenses include travel, going out to dinner, clothes, and so on. It includes the "fun" stuff—even some of the bigger splurges you might make, like a European vacation. If there was another 2008 financial crisis or Great Depression, your discretionary expenses are the types of spending you'd be willing to give up for a while. They're not *necessary* to live; they're purchases you make at your discretion, because you want them.

Let's say that Joe spends an average of $100,000 annually on discretionary expenses. At a glance, this looks like a problem. When you add Joe's fixed gap of -$70,000 to his discretionary expenses of -$100,000, we can see Joe's *total income need* equals $170,000.

Joe is retired and doesn't want to work anymore—but he needs $170,000. As it stands, Joe does not appear to be financially independent. What can he do?

Luckily, Joe is going to benefit from the second layer of the diagram!

ACHIEVING FINANCIAL INDEPENDENCE
WITH YOUR INVESTABLE ASSETS

Investable Assets $10M

Emergency Allocation $70K	Fixed Gap Allocation $2.33M	Discretionary Allocation $3.33M	Other Allocation $4.27M
12-month Fixed Gap	$70K + .03 = $2.33M	$100K + .03 = $3.33M	
Hold liquid investments that will cover 12-month expense gap	Generate 3% income stream to cover $70K annual fixed gap	Generate $100K discretionary income, assuming 3% withdrawal rate on growing principal	Grow portfolio for aspirational goals
LOW RISK	**LOW RISK**	**MODERATE RISK**	**HIGH RISK**

The second layer of the diagram has a box labeled "Investable Assets." In that box goes the total amount of investable assets you own. Between Joe's disciplined saving and investing, as well his inheritance from his parents, he has $10 million worth of assets to write down in that box.

This box also has two branches coming off to the left and right of the "Investable Assets" box, and under each branch is a description of funds needed for different purposes. We're going to call each of these "buckets." The left branch is going to represent the money you need to earn from your assets to cover your basic needs. "Wait—my basic needs?" you might be thinking. "Isn't that what I just figured out with the fixed income gap bit?" Close, but not quite.

The first bucket hanging under the left arm is labeled "Emergency Allocation," and we would put this in the category of a basic need. Think of this as the money you would need to be able to survive six to twelve months of your fixed gap, if there was an emergency. In Joe's case, he'd need $70,000 to make it through a year and keep his lights on. (Remember? That's his yearly fixed income gap.) So, we'll note $70,000 in Joe's emergency bucket.

As a side note, we can't recommend highly enough the wisdom of the emergency bucket. Imagine your furnace breaks, you need a new car, or you're slapped with a large medical bill. If a crisis were to hit, you don't want to have to pull all of your fixed expenses from your investment port-folio at an inopportune time in the stock market. Without that emergency bucket, you could quickly find yourself in a precarious position.

For your emergency bucket, we recommend holdings in cash, savings accounts, checking accounts, money market accounts, or short-term CDs. You still want to be earn-ing interest on a sum as large as an entire year's worth of expenses, but for an emergency bucket, you also need funds that are readily available. All of those recommended investment formats are considered "liquid" and they could be quickly accessed in an emergency—but they'll still be earning you interest.

Now let's deal with the second bucket on that left arm. Next to "Emergency Allocation" is a bucket labeled "Fixed Gap Allocation." Remember how Joe needs $70,000 annually, just to meet his fixed expenses? That's his "Fixed Income Gap." "Fixed Gap Allocation" represents the money that Joe has allocated to meet that fixed gap. He'll need to earn that money from his most secure investments, to cover his fixed income gap on an annual, reliable basis.

What are secure investments? We'll go over this in greater

depth in the next chapter, but essentially, they're investments that you can generally count on to produce a predictable return. CDs, treasuries, municipals, and annuities, for example, might be considered very secure, although what counts as a "secure" investment is often dependent on the current economic situation and what tools you might have at your disposal. In any case, Joe doesn't want to have to worry about volatility in the stock market when he's looking for money to cover his fixed expenses. He needs to make at least $70,000 in annual interest from *secure* investments to cover his fixed gap.

Fortunately, Joe has assets to pull from. How much of that money does Joe need to put in secure investments, then, to give him a steady cash flow of $70,000 of annual interest? To arrive at this number, we'll do a little math: divide the fixed need by the interest rate you're earning from your secure investments. Joe is earning 3 percent on his secure investments, written as 0.03, so his equation is: $70,000 ÷ 0.03. That equals $2,333,333, which, at 3 percent, will generate $70,000 annually. So, Joe needs about $2.3 million in secure investments to get him the money he needs for his fixed expenses. (Remember this is a basic evaluation and does not consider the influence of inflation and taxes.)

Let's review: Joe has $70,000 in his "Emergency Allocation" bucket. He has $2.3 million in his "Fixed Gap Allocation" bucket. That means he has $7.6 million remaining in his portfolio to be used for discretionary spending. As we've discovered, Joe is a smart operator, so in one of the buckets on the arm extending from the right of the "Investable Assets" bubble, Joe is going to put enough assets to cover his $100,000 discretionary spending need.

We'll do some more math to figure out, once again, how much Joe needs to cover his $100,000 discretionary expenses. Joe has set up a balanced investment portfolio, and decides that an annual withdrawal rate of 3 percent would be reasonable to meet his $100,000 discretionary expenses while allowing the portfolio to continue growing. How much, then, does he need in the balanced portfolio to cover that amount?

To determine that number, we divide the discretionary expense need, by the percentage of withdrawal. In Joe's case, that looks like: $100,000 ÷ 0.03 = $3.33 million. (We'll talk more about a well-balanced portfolio in our next chapter.) At this withdrawal rate and historical market returns, it is reasonable to assume the discretionary expenses would be covered for life.

At this point, we can conclude that Joe meets the qualifications for our earlier definition of Financial Independence. He is able to make modest, sustainable withdrawals from his assets to cover his fixed income gap *and* his discretionary spending. What's more, Joe is also building up assets that he can leave as an inheritance. For example, he's covering his discretionary expenses by withdrawing 3 percent from the invested portfolio with $3.33 million—but if he were to die, that $3.33 million would all be passed on.

So, the first three buckets represent funds that are needed for *your* use, during your lifetime. It's these three buckets that make work optional. However, the funds that make your financial independence possible will also function as investments that you can pass on as an inheritance. For many people, covering your needs *and* providing an inheritance is the true definition of financial independence.

For some people, financial independence means even more than that—and that's where we'll start discussing our fourth bucket. Some people want to work to build their wealth until they can accomplish not only a legacy for their families, but a legacy for their communities. Let's return to Joe and see what he does with that fourth bucket.

Joe still has $4.27 million left. We'll name Joe's final bucket "Other Allocation." This bucket represents money that is above and beyond what Joe needs to live on—it's "icing on the cake." With this money, Joe can pursue some amazing aspirations—including (and perhaps most importantly) setting up his legacy of an inheritance. He might choose to give this money to charity, establish a foundation, or support an organization that he believes in. Or, he might simply choose to leave a large gift to his family for their use and perpetuation. You can think of the fourth bucket as the "Aspirations" or "Legacy" bucket.

Given what we've discovered through inputting all of Joe's numbers, we can conclude that he is not only in a strong position of financial independence, he's also in a position to pass it on.[26] He has enough cash flow coming in from his fixed income and secure investments to cover his basic needs. He's also covering his discretionary spending by taking modest withdrawals from his investable assets. Rather than draining his assets to cover his spending, he's actually maintaining his assets. In fact, the $7.6 million which he's invested in higher growth investment opportunities is likely *growing* his assets beyond what he's living

---

26 Note: Inflation and taxes are not considered in this example, but are also important variables to consider when making decisions.

on. Joe has more than enough, and is in a great position to bless his loved ones by passing on his wealth.

If we were to input different numbers and discover that there wasn't enough income from fixed income sources and/or investable assets to cover the emergency bucket and fixed income gap—then that person would *not* be in a position of financial independence.

Now, if you are a child who's inherited millions of dollars, that can feel like a ridiculous statement. It's not, though; we sometimes see people simply *drain* the assets to cover their large discretionary expenses, rather than maintain and grow the assets, like Joe is doing. That's the situation where second, third, and fourth generations fail to pass the wealth on; they end up spending it away.

That's not what we want for our kids, and we're guessing that's not what you'd want for your kids either. Learning the true meaning of financial independence, as well as the difference between rich versus wealthy, is an important piece of financial literacy to understand, if children are expected to pass on their wealth to future generations.

From our experience, everyone either intentionally or unintentionally operates according to this model, making different decisions about their buckets. If a person is in their working years, they might logically live within their general wages or less. In that case, any bonuses, gifts from grandparents, or birthday monies are put into the discretionary expenses bucket or into long-term assets. However, sometimes the model can highlight questionable decision-making, like putting the emergency bucket funds in a high yield bond fund for the sake of a higher return; that's not actually a wise choice.

For these reasons, the diagram can serve as a useful education: it can provide a sense of what it takes to create the money you require to live on, and point out the wisest strategies for each bucket. The diagram can also be applied as a tool to evaluate whether or not you're financially independent. It can highlight next steps in pursuing your financial goals, like building up the emergency bucket. Finally, by identifying clear goals, the diagram can help—on a basic level—overcome the emotional biases that often negatively impact the portfolio construction.

GOALS-BASED APPROACH TO MONEY MANAGEMENT

We've talked about goals-based money management on a very simple level—like, on the Mason jars level. We're now going to discuss how that concept should be understood with greater complexity, and ultimately help you determine your financial strategies.

In the diagram titled, "Achieving Financial Independence with Your Investable Assets," we depict different buckets to discuss how to achieve financial independence. Those buckets have different priorities. Joe's most important bucket to fill is his emergency fund bucket. His next priority bucket is his fixed gap bucket, because that's how he keeps his utilities working. From there, his third priority bucket is his discretionary expenses bucket, and finally, he invests in his aspirations bucket.

Those different buckets are a way to illustrate the concept

of a goals-based money management strategy. The basic premise of **goals-based money management is assigning your highest priorities with the lowest risk investments.** This is another important financial literacy concept which will lead to wise financial management.

You can visualize these different buckets, with their different investment approaches almost like pyramids.

GOALS-BASED INVESTING APPROACH

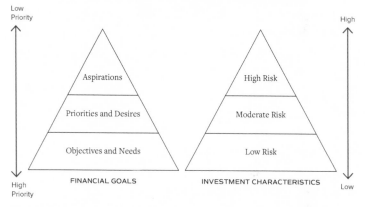

At the base of your financial health is how you provide for your "Objectives and Needs": your fixed income gap and your emergency bucket. You've got to cover those needs first before you do anything else; it's your **highest priority**. The money devoted to covering that particular goal needs to be easily accessible, in a **low-risk** investment.

After establishing a foundation which covers those financial *needs,* you can devote money toward your "Priorities and Desires," i.e., your discretionary income. Your discretionary income is money you don't necessarily need to spend, so your investment strategy for that goal changes accordingly: you can take **more risks** and the funds don't need to be immediately accessible.

The area which can accommodate the **highest risk** in investment strategy is the bucket devoted to your financial "Aspirations." These financial goals are the ones that are furthest off and don't need to be accessible until a specific time frame in the future.

As described in Joe's example, he made sure that all of the assets which were supplying his emergency bucket were low risk and easily accessible. That's a goal-based money management strategy: that particular bucket has a particular goal (to help him out in case of an emergency), and his investment strategy is set up to meet that goal.

If you get this goals-based money management strategy wrong, you set yourself up for unnecessary complications. If Joe's car breaks down and he suddenly needs to buy a new one, but his emergency fund is all tied up in the stock market, he's got an issue. Conversely, if he's trying to save for his retirement by putting all of his money into short-term CDs with a relatively low interest rate, he's missing out on his opportunity to maximize long-term growth.

In our industry, people often talk about goals-based investing, and building a layered portfolio. While we don't use that exact terminology with our kids, we approach the conversation with them in a similar way. Our use of the Mason jars in distributing their allowance is a basic illustration which will eventually help them understand the need for a layered portfolio. There are different goals attached to each jar, and different time horizons associated with when they'll access it.

HUMAN CAPITAL VERSUS FINANCIAL CAPITAL

Human capital and financial capital are key aspects of financial literacy that should be understood. **Financial capital is pretty straightforward: it's the money you possess.** Human capital describes a person's earning *potential*. **Human capital is the present value of future earnings, and should be thought of as an investable asset.** Any effort made to increase future wages could be considered an investment in human capital. Debt should also be considered in terms of human capital. Going into debt to get an education is essentially investing in your human capital.

HUMAN CAPITAL VS FINANCIAL CAPITAL

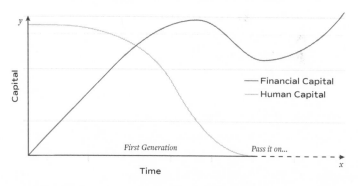

This concept can be illustrated in a graph, where the *y* axis represents capital, and the *x* axis represents time. When time is at zero, the line for *financial* capital is also effectively zero. We can tell you: our youngest son Jack, as a three-year-old, is not making any money. He has zero financial capital.

Early in life, most people do not have much financial capital to speak of.

However, early in life, *human* capital is sky-high, and it will remain high throughout a person's youth. As you go through school, gain work experience, and go to college, you are making consistent investments in your human capital. When you first start working as — let's say, a twenty-two-year-old — your human capital is as high as it gets. You are skilled, educated, and have a lifetime's worth of work to put into a company.

With each year you work, though, you presumably have one less year of work to give. Your human capital — your earning potential — falls a little more every year. By the time you stop working, your human capital will have diminished. Imagine a construction worker's human capital when he's young: he might be strong, energetic, and can work fourteen-hour days. However, particularly in a physical profession, as a person's body ages, their human capital inevitably decreases.

Notice though, that as human capital falls, *financial* capital grows. That is, it grows *if* you have saved and invested for the future. Ideally, financial capital increases with time and offsets the loss of your human capital. Typically it peaks toward the end of your life, when your human capital is declining. As healthcare demands come into play, you will see the financial capital dip. However, in an ideal world, your financial capital would continue to grow exponentially as you get older. That way, you could live off the interest of your wealth without diving into the principal.

If you fail to preserve your financial capital, however, you risk forfeiting your quality of life when your human capital is diminished. Let's say you don't save any money at all throughout your life. You make—and spend—$250,000 a year. Chances are you lived well. However, you may find yourself suddenly seventy-five years old with no savings. You have no financial capital, other than social security income. Not only would you lack financial capital, but you would no longer have the ability to make more money due to your low human capital.

But, let's say you do practice diligence in saving money and at the end of your life, you possess wealth to pass on. What happens to that financial capital when your human capital expires and you pass away? You can get a picture of this visually by referencing back to the graph—note the dash mark and inflection point of financial capital in the chart. Remember the power of time when money is given a chance to grow and gain compound interest? That time factor will benefit the second generation if you manage an efficient transfer of wealth. Your children and grandchildren can continue to increase that financial capital which will start to experience exponential growth from the effects of compounding interest.

You have the potential to provide your second and third generations with a great deal of momentum in their financial capital as they're just getting started, opening new doors for them to invest in their human capital. *This* is a picture of passing it on: your inheritance has the potential to change the financial profile for the next generation—and indeed, the entire course of their lives.

Our advice: as you go through life, really consider how your decisions affect these long-term glide paths. Understanding human capital versus financial capital is at the core of financial education.

CASH FLOW

Imagine that you sit down to play a game of Monopoly. The game gets off to a good start for you—you land on multiple valuable properties and you're able to put together the cash to buy most of them. Finally, you land on the most valuable property of all: Boardwalk. You already own its neighbor, Park Place, and if you could manage to buy Boardwalk, you'd have a monopoly. If you put houses or hotels on the properties, you'd likely start dominating the game.

There's one problem: you've already spent all your available cash when you purchased the other properties in your hand. Although you *look* like the wealthiest player with all your properties, you have no cash flow.

No problem: as you might in the real world, you take out the Monopoly version of a loan. You flip over several properties in your hand, collect their mortgage value, and use the cash to buy Boardwalk. All those mortgaged properties will now be useless until you can pay back the "loan," but you assume that won't take long. After all—you now own Park Place *and* Boardwalk!

Still—that optimistic future can only come to pass with more *cash*. If cash flow dries up, even the most impressive financial assets can be lost. For this reason, successful companies and successful wealth builders need to create a steady stream of cash flow.

"Cash flow" describes the income generated from your assets on a periodic basis. In Monopoly, for instance, you know that you're going to collect two hundred dollars every time you pass "Go." In the real world, if your assets are producing a steady stream of income which is available to you to spend, you have positive cash flow. However, if that money is tied up in inaccessible assets, or delayed, you have poor cash flow.

Speaking of the real world, let's take this board game scenario and drop it into reality. Imagine that it's 2007, and Ryan is in the Monopoly business: he does commercial real estate, buying properties and renting them out. He extends his available cash to pursue aggressive growth which he's confident will pay off. He makes smart investments in undeveloped land, venture capitalism, and maximizes his 401(k) contribution. On paper, Ryan is unquestionably wealthy — even though most of his net worth isn't readily accessible.

And then, the 2008 crisis hits.

One by one, the business tenants in Ryan's expensive highrise buildings start telling him they can't afford their rent. Eventually, most of them leave and Ryan loses the majority of his rental income. The businesses he invested in as a venture capitalist flounder; many fail. No one can afford to build on the undeveloped land he purchased. He's responsible for a couple million in debt and he doesn't have the cash needed to meet the payments.

Consider the opportunity cost that comes when you don't have cash flow. In the 2008 financial crisis, for instance, the markets turned into a fire sale. Valuable properties and stocks were being sold for a steal. A commercial real estate developer like Ryan might have seen all kinds of properties that would make incredible investments—but if there's no cash flow, there's no capability to take advantage of those investments. People who maintain available cash flow have the opportunity to take advantage of these investments; they also don't have to desperately sell off their assets during a financial crisis. They can ride the roller coaster, sustain their investments, and take advantage of the opportunities that come their way.

Some of the biggest businesses in our country—companies as well established as General Electric—have floundered because of their lack of cash flow. In fact, one article said that GE's reboot in the end of 2019 came almost entirely because they got a better handle on their cash flow.[27] If cash flow can pose a challenge to some of the biggest companies in our country, it can certainly pose a challenge to families as well—even those with considerable wealth.

As you might have gathered from our financial independence illustration, cash flow is at the heart of a successful charge toward financial independence. This point was made personal to us when we recently refinanced our home mortgage. The bank wasn't interested in our brokerage or 401(k) statements, but they *did* want paycheck stubs, W-2s, and multiple years of tax returns. They cared about cash flow, not net worth.

Achieving wealth isn't the same as having the cash flow to

27 Samaha, Lee. "Here's Why General Electric Stock Is Soaring."
    Nasdaq, November 4, 2019. https://www.nasdaq.com/articles/
    heres-why-general-electric-stock-is-soaring-2019-11-04.

do what you want to do. You need take-home income—that's what we mean by cash—for housing, groceries, car maintenance, and to pay your debts.

Simply put, when you have reliable cash flow, you're able to take advantage of opportunities. When all your net worth is tied up in inaccessible assets, you risk missing out on some of those opportunities and may likely experience additional stress.

So, what are some practical ways to maintain a reliable, steady stream of cash flow? The most reliable stream of income for most people comes from their W-2 income, pensions, or Social Security. However, if you own your own business or have stopped working, that income stream needs to come from your assets—ideally in a way that doesn't deplete their worth, but sustains them. Creating several different sources of passive income is one successful cash flow strategy we've seen. Real estate, dividend paying stocks, and fixed income investments are common sources of passive income which can produce reliable cash flow.

Basically, cash flow is an important element to managing wealth and important to keep in mind all the time!

SPENDING HABITS

Speaking of cash flow, there's a fantastic board game called "Cash Flow" produced by Richard Kiyosaki, author of the popular book *Rich Dad Poor Dad*. Along the edge of the game board are pictures of dreams that can only be fulfilled through having great wealth, things like heli-skiing or traveling the world. The goal of the game is to build enough wealth to be able to buy your dream. You do that through lots of small, strategic decisions.

This set-up is brilliant, because all other financial decisions are weighed based on how they help you meet those long-term goals. Building up passive income is a winning strategy, as is building up an investment portfolio. On the other hand, big purchases which depreciate quickly, like Ferraris or yachts, take you further away from achieving those long-term goals. Game players learn that they have to save smart, spend smart, and invest smart, if they want to achieve the long-term dreams.

The game's focus on long-term financial goals is counter-cultural. America is not a country that generally encourages financial restraint. If marketers had their way, we would all operate via impulse buys. Most of us get a constant barrage of marketing which makes us want to hurry and buy! Buy and enjoy! Then hurry and buy again! But it's the *long-term* vision of financial goals that will ultimately make you and your kids more successful when they spend money.

Here's why this matters, especially for people who are starting off wealthy: if you spend your money mainly on the experiences of "today"—on the house, the cars, the activities, and so on—yet fail to save for the future, your estate will not last for future generations. Your children will have no idea how to operate with long-term goals or future generations in mind, and the money will evaporate.

For people with more modest means, failure to consider the future could even make you a burden to your children later on. If you prioritize your kids' spending needs for most of your adult life, you run the risk of waking up as an empty-nester at fifty, and only then start thinking about retirement. Remember our example of Bill, when we discussed compound interest? It's not a great strategy to start saving for retirement at age fifty. With little to no retirement savings, who will end up caring for you in your old age? The Jet Ski may have seemed like a good idea when you were forty and your teenager was fourteen, but not when your adult children are staring at brochures of seedy retirement homes and wishing you had thought more of your own future.

When your children start earning W-2 income, help them shape good early habits of how they save, as well as how they spend. Here's the challenge: short-term considerations are almost always going to feel more compelling than long-term goals. It's going to be hard to convince your kids to save up for some abstract long-term goal, when they'd rather spend their money going out to a movie with friends.

Sometimes, spending *is* the right choice. Seeing a movie with friends, signing up for another activity, taking the field trip to Washington, D.C.—those are all experiences that we want our kids to have, and that we would be happy to spend money on. But, just like the game teaches, kids need to learn that their spending habits have an impact on whether or not they can achieve their long-term dreams.

Given the complicated considerations that need to be weighed with most financial decisions, there's no one formula which will help you determine the right spending decision every time. However, by helping your kids develop the values we've already highlighted—particularly delayed gratification and goal-setting—they'll be better equipped to thrive in many areas of life, and certainly in the area of wise spending.

FINANCIAL SMARTS HELP YOU PASS IT ON

All of the concepts discussed in this chapter ultimately inform *strategy*:

- If you know the power of compound interest, you can use it to your benefit, allowing time to do the heavy-lifting of wealth building.
- If you understand what it means to be financially independent, you're less at risk for blowing through an inheritance, and more apt to work toward building up your family's estate as a family steward.
- By understanding that at the core of financial literacy is financial capital versus human capital, you have a better sense of how your decisions will affect your long-term financial trajectory as your human capital diminishes.
- Understanding the importance of cash flow can help you support a business, stay on top of your debts, and maintain a good credit rating. It opens you up to take advantage of opportunities and gives you needed flexibility.
- By balancing short-term spending needs with long-term goals, you're more likely to achieve those long-term goals and be strategic in how you get there.

Because of how directly each piece of financial literacy knowledge informs strategy, an understanding of these concepts will directly impact your ability (and your children's ability) to pass it on. The more financial smarts you have, the more capable you will be in forming a strategy for building and maintaining your wealth.

Don't miss the importance of values in getting there. Many of the concepts in this chapter rely on those family stewardship values of long-term goal setting and delayed gratification. You *invest early* for a long-term goal like retirement, then *wait* to earn compound interest. You do *long-term goal setting* to consider your state of financial independence and ensure you'll be able to pass your wealth on eventually. You keep the *long view* in mind when considering how best to invest your human capital. You practice *delayed gratification* and consider *long-term goals* when spending your money.

Although it's never too late to pass these concepts on to your children, they'll be most successful if they get them early. Anna's future as an athlete will benefit from her early years of building strength and flexibility in gymnastics. Similarly, your children will have decades of successful financial habits if they learn these lessons and engender these values early on.

CHAPTER FIVE

FINANCIAL LITERACY: INVESTING, INSURANCE, DEBT, AND TAXES

"An investment in knowledge pays the best dividends."

BENJAMIN FRANKLIN

A COLLEGE KID INVESTOR: ROGER NARRATES

When I was still pursuing my engineering degree in college, I decided to start dabbling in stock investments. Now that I manage stocks for a living, I've realized there's an enormous amount to understand about wise portfolio building, but back then, I was overconfident. I had a plan, and it seemed like a good way to make a lot of money quickly—so I went for it.

At the time, during the height of the tech boom, I was working as an intern for a tech company that made semi-

FINANCIAL LITERACY: INVESTING, INSURANCE, DEBT, AND TAXES · 139

conductors. It was an exciting time—people were becoming rich overnight with the explosion of tech stock valuations. Every morning when I arrived at work, I would observe the Humvees and Ferraris in the parking lot which the executives drove. The connection seemed obvious to me: clearly, tech stocks were the path to riches. That impression was confirmed by stories I heard on the news, reporting that "tech stocks are hot!"

In my field as an engineer, I was exposed to a great deal of technology, and I figured I had some better understanding than most about the value they might hold. I spent almost all my long-term savings on those tech stocks, and watched for the values to skyrocket. Initially, the stocks did increase in value. I saw my money double and thought investing was easy. I gave myself a pat on the back for my brilliant strategy.

Then, the tech bubble burst. All the gains I'd made evaporated, and the stocks' values plunged down far below the value where I'd bought them.

It was a rookie mistake. At the time, I had no working knowledge of the fact that the market goes through cycles. Sectors can be winners for a period of time and then become losers. In hindsight, I had not done enough fundamental evaluation of my investment decisions. I'd put all my eggs in one basket, and then the basket dropped.

I learned some valuable lessons from that experience though. First, diversification is a valuable tool. Owning a concentrated portfolio made me vulnerable to a specific sector going out of favor. Sometimes concentrated positions *do* turn out to be big winners, and stockholders gain enormous amounts on their investment. But it can just as easily go the other way. With diversification, i.e., investing in a wide variety of stock holdings, comes more reliable long-term positive outcomes. We're going to talk more about that in a second.

I also learned that stock investing is more complicated than I'd initially realized. There are many factors to consider: timing, the big picture, the state of the economy, the type of investment holdings, and so on. The experience incentivized me to educate myself about all the variables to consider when building an investment portfolio.

There's a lot to learn about investments, along with other major areas of finance, like debt, insurance, and taxes. Many books have been written about each topic, and we're not going to try to relay all the particulars of each one here. However, we want to make sure readers of our book have some basic financial literacy in each. You yourself have already become a family steward—that's why you are reading this book, to pass it on successfully. This chapter may function as a refresher for you and covers the financial literacy points your children should know. We'd like to try to help your children avoid similar "rookie" mistakes, give them some foundational knowledge, and set them up to better pursue the kind of deeper information that will best fit your unique family situation.

We'll be talking about investments, insurance, debt, and taxes in this chapter. Each area can lead to a major drain on your investments if handled poorly:

- If you don't **invest** wisely, you essentially give your money to inflation or take on unnecessary risk.

- If you don't protect your assets with **insurance**, you're vulnerable to unexpected circumstances or risks.
- If you don't handle your **debt** well, you lose your money to creditors.
- If you aren't smart about how you manage your **taxes**, you give a disproportionate amount of your money away to the government.

In other words, failure to achieve basic financial literacy in each of these areas means you're making the decision to *not* "pass it on." At least—you won't be passing it on to the people you love.

However, each area of money management can also be a source of growth, when handled wisely. Yes, even debt can help your estate grow in the long run, if you're smart about it! Let's start with the most obvious area where you can grow your wealth: Investments.

INVESTMENTS

"You give a little; you get a little." That's one way to sum up the goal of investment strategies: you put money into an opportunity that, you expect, will give you a good return on your investment and help your money grow. Some areas of investment are viewed as more secure, but also promise smaller growth. Others have the potential for greater growth, but also pose greater risk. We'll discuss these different categories of investments, along with some fundamental concepts like asset allocation, risk, volatility, and some good investing rules of thumb.

CATEGORIES OF INVESTMENTS

As a reminder, the investment opportunities that offer the highest gains also pose the greatest risk. On the flip side, the safest investments usually offer lower rates of return. Let's take a look at the different categories of investments to understand how each one generally functions and can work with the others to create balance in your portfolio.

The basic categories of investments include cash, fixed income, and equities. The investments listed first are the safest, and usually the most conservative in their rates of return. The investments listed last are the most risky, but also offer the most potential gain.

- **Cash Equivalents:** Money invested in cash equivalents is typically held in savings accounts and insured up to the FDIC limits. This is your "safe" money and the most liquid and readily available.
- **Fixed income:** Fixed income instruments are categorized by their reliable rates of return and/or steady stream of income they produce. This category includes certificates of deposit (CDs), treasury bills, corporate bonds, mortgage-backed securities, and municipal bonds, etc.
- **Equities:** Equities refers to stock investments. Generally, bigger companies (large-cap) are considered lower-risk investments, and smaller companies (small-cap) are higher risk, but also have the potential for larger gains. Traditional equity asset classes include: large-cap stocks, mid-cap stocks, small-cap stocks, and international stocks.

ASSET ALLOCATION AND DIVERSIFICATION

Asset allocation is the intersection of art and science when it comes to managing wealth and it is often said to be the most important investment decision. Some scholarly research suggests that approximately *90 percent* of portfolio returns will be determined by how an investor chooses to allocate.[28] That's significant!

Think back to our "buckets" illustration when we were explaining how to determine your financial independence. If you have some funds in savings accounts for emergencies, some funds in fixed income assets for your regular expenses, and some funds in stocks for more long-term goals—then you've allocated your assets. Different money for different goals in different assets equals asset allocation—that is, on a broad, macro level.

However, in the investing community, "asset allocation" usually means something much more specific related to a portfolio. Here's an example of how asset allocation might look in terms of an investment portfolio: let's say you put 20 percent of your capital in large-caps; 20 percent in mid-caps; 15 percent in international; 5 percent in small-caps; and 40 percent in fixed income.[29] You've allocated your assets across a number of different types of investment categories. (Note: these numbers are *not* meant to be prescriptive; they're meant to provide an example only.)

---

28 Brinson, Gary P., L. Randolph Hood & Gilbert L. Beebower (1995) Determinants of Portfolio Performance, Financial Analysts Journal, 51:1, 133-138, DOI: 10.2469/faj. v51.n1.1869

29 Large caps, mid-caps, and small caps all refer to company size, or, "market capitalization." Large caps refer to large companies, which post large market capitalization; mid-caps refer to mid-size companies; small caps refer to small companies.

Now, why would asset allocation be such an important step? Here's why: when people invest their money, they are hoping to maximize their gains, and minimize their losses. Deep down, we all want a guarantee that we'll profit from our investments.

In 1952, a Nobel Laureate named Harry Markowitz introduced an investing theory called "the efficient frontier." Basically, he determined the percentages for asset allocation that **most consistently resulted in maximized returns for the level of risk assumed.**[30] His theory is now a cornerstone of investment strategies. Once a person's level of risk comfort is determined, assets are divvied up into different asset classes according to the optimal percentage recommendations put forward by the efficient frontier theory.

Once you have decided where to put your money via asset allocation, you're going to want to invest in a wide variety of offerings within each asset category. That's **diversification.** Broadly speaking, a diverse financial picture means you've put your proverbial eggs in lots of different baskets; **you're spreading out your assets across a wide range of investment types.** When you diversify your asset allocation, it's like you're spreading the weight out around a boat: there's more balance, increased ballast, and your craft is more stable. Adequate diversification equals less volatility.

Let's take, for example, the assets that make up your fixed income stream. It would be a mistake to rely on a single corporate bond to provide that entire fixed income stream. What if the company defaults? Your supposedly reliable

---

30 Ganti, Akhilesh. "Efficient Frontier Definition." Investopedia. Investopedia, April 1, 2019. https://www.investopedia.com/terms/e/efficientfrontier.asp.

income stream which you use to pay your bills is no longer producing the income you need. A *diversified* fixed income portfolio, on the other hand, may include several different vehicles: corporate bonds, U.S. treasuries, CDs, and mutual funds, for instance.

Within your equity portfolio, we can understand diversification more specifically: you're picking a variety of stocks within each asset class. Here's why this is a good idea: if a particular sector of the market plummets—like when the tech bubble burst, or when the banking industry was hit hard in 2008—a diversified portfolio can still hang tough. So, within large-caps, you might own stock in Microsoft (software), Johnson & Johnson (pharma), JPMorgan Chase (banking), and Berkshire Hathaway (diversified). If pharmaceuticals start to fall because of new federal regulations, your portfolio's *diversification* may protect your investments from taking too big a hit.

Maybe this seems like a basic point. "Yeah, yeah, yeah," you might be thinking. "Of course I know to diversify." But here's where we sometimes see people go astray: often, people are inclined to focus their investments in an area where they have the most expertise, like Roger initially did with tech. That can be an easy misstep.

Let's say a contractor is inclined to invest heavily in the area of construction. He knows the machines, he knows the product companies, he might even know what neighborhoods are up-and-coming—so, he invests in what he knows is quality. Sometimes, a person like this might *think* he's diversified his assets. Perhaps he owns his own company, earns additional income by flipping houses, and has invested in ten different publicly traded construction companies. But if all his assets depend on the success of one particular area of business—construction—that's not diversification.

Consider the housing crisis during the great recession: one of the biggest areas hit was construction. If our contractor guy relies on construction for his W-2 income, his capital gains, and real-estate profits, he's totally dependent on the success of the construction market for his livelihood. When that market tanks, his assets collectively tank as well. Although it's counter-intuitive, it's actually wiser for people to invest in an area of business that's *dissimilar* to the source of their W-2 income. In sum: you need diversity in categories of investments *and* across economic sectors.

RISK VERSUS VOLATILITY: ROGER NARRATES

Back in the 1600s, Dutch commerce was defined by Tulip Mania. Rare tulip bulbs were considered more valuable than fine gems or great works of art. People traded acres of land for a single bulb. Then, the market abruptly evaporated. A bulb that was worth a fortune one day was worth almost nothing only days later. Many people who had staked their fortunes and properties on these valuable bulbs were ruined in a day.

I experienced an evaporating market firsthand with my childhood baseball card collection. One year, I made it my goal to form "a full set," meaning I would have every card that was made that year. I bought pack after pack of cards, trying to get every single player represented in my collection. I was confident that my full set would perpetually appreciate in value, and eventually make me a tidy profit.

It didn't, and it's not. I think that full set is worth approximately zero dollars today.

Tulip Mania and my baseball card collection are good examples of what we would classify as *risk*. **Risk** describes an investment that has the possibility for great growth—but also **could result in a total loss of capital**, meaning it ends up being worth nothing. Risky investments are a gamble.

Volatility, on the other hand, **describes the day-to-day or month-to-month movement in the stock market**. If you went to sell something on any given day, it might sell for less than what you paid for it, but there's still *value*. (Remember: risk could lead to zero value.) Over a longer period of time, history shows that the general market trend is upward. By tolerating the up-and-down volatility that you see over time in the stock market, patient investors usually see positive long-term rates of return.

In short: *volatility* is to be expected, and you can weather it through patience, asset allocation, and diversification. *Risk* is something that should only be taken on with great care, and a lot of thought.

Some conservative investors might decide they don't want to deal with either risk *or* volatility, and would rather put all their capital in the safest investments, like savings accounts. However, if you were to put all your capital in such safe investments, you won't see enough of a return to even keep up with inflation. Some risk *is* necessary.

Aggressive investors, on the other hand, might want to go after the "hot" stocks that seem like they're going to give you the highest rate of return, just like Roger did as a college student with the tech stocks. Imagining yourself in a Ferrari or a Humvee makes a risky investment strategy seem worth it! But here's a simple mathematical equation to keep in mind when you're evaluating risk in your portfolio: **whenever a stock drops 50 percent, it needs to climb back up *100 percent*.**

For example, if you have $2.00, and it goes down 50 percent to $1.00, then it has to rebound *100 percent* to get back to even. That's expecting a lot. In the case of especially risky investments, there's a possibility that the 100 percent rebound may never happen at all. The market for some products, like video rental stores, can simply vanish.

When you're considering how much risk you're going to put into your portfolio, consider the "down-50-up-100" rule. You can minimize both risk and volatility, once again, through asset allocation and diversification.

PAY YOURSELF FIRST

We've just laid out a lot of technical discussion about asset allocation, diversification, risk, and volatility—all of those investment tools are ultimately ways to minimize risk and optimize gain. But there's another strategy you can use for investment which is far less technical: at the end of the day, **you need to be committed to investing in yourself first.**

There's an old "investment" rule that you should invest approximately 10 percent in your own future before investing in anything else—and if you can do more than 10 percent, even better. Before treating yourself to that next latte, you pay yourself first by putting 10 percent aside for long-term savings and investing.

We have a friend who managed a comfortable, early retirement after working in a blue-collar job for his entire career, exactly because he paid himself first. Early in his working days, an older colleague gave him some gruff advice: "Every time you get paid, you've got to put 10 percent of that in your 401(k). You've got to do it." Our friend took his advice, and it paid off. He's now taking camping trips and hiking with his kids, enjoying his retirement after paying himself first.

As our friend experienced, one of the most valuable and easy ways to set this up is through a 401(k). You can set up an automatic 10 percent withdrawal from your gross pay, pre-tax, which is invested in a retirement account for your future. The remaining 90 percent of your paycheck is yours to live on, eat on, and invest in other priorities. But by paying yourself first, you're investing in your own future.

The "Pay Yourself First" concept is especially important when you think about the importance of building up your human capital—i.e., your income-earning potential. Human capital is its own asset class. When you invest in your health or education, you increase your human capital.

If you invest liquid money into human capital for your own care and development, you increase the time variable of how long you'll be able to earn money, which can lead to powerful financial gains down the road. You might also be protecting yourself from losing your job or letting your health fall apart, which would obviously hurt your earning potential.

Pay yourself first—through savings for the future *and* by investing in your own potential.

INSURANCE

Insurance is about protecting your capital—both your financial assets, and even more importantly, your human capital. Although we're going to discuss several types of insurance, we'll start the conversation with life insurance.

When looking to protect your family, a good starting point for thinking about life insurance should address where you're at with your human capital. We've defined human capital as the present value of your future earnings capacity. Typically when you're young, you have *more* human capital, and less financial capital. When you're older, that ratio flips. Your insurance should cover your human capital: you usually need more when you're young, and less when you're old.

There are two main types of life insurance: term and permanent. Term is more common, so we'll start there.

TERM INSURANCE

Term life insurance covers you for a certain amount of time, such as ten, twenty, or thirty years; you can also select a policy like "term to age sixty-five" which provides coverage up until you turn 65, or another specified age. You may also buy "renewable" term, which means at the end of the duration you may renew without a new health review; however, at renewal the premium would still rise. These policies are usually *cheaper* than permanent insurance, like whole life or universal life policies. Since the policies cover shorter spans of time, and mostly cover young healthy people, insurance carriers know that the policies won't typically need to be paid out. They can therefore afford to make them less expensive.

Term policies should be *need-based*: a term policy should cover the various expenses that you might need to pay during the span of time covered by the term. Their main function is to **protect your family and cover debt**.

For example, let's say we're talking about a couple who have young kids and they're just getting into their prime working years. We'll call them Sarah and David. David is thirty-five and intends to work for another thirty years, making an average of $100,000 per year. There are plenty of expenses to cover in this phase of life: mortgage payments, childcare, future college funds, and so on. If anything were to happen to David, his life insurance policy would ideally enable Sarah to still have the ability to cover all those expenses while maintaining her current lifestyle.

Therefore, when the two of them look into life insurance for David, he should get a policy that reflects his human capital—his *potential future earnings*—at age thirty-five. He needs to be insured for all the money that would no longer be available to his family in the future, should anything happen to him.

So how much is "enough"? "Enough" is going to depend heavily on your situation in life. If you're married without children, you may only need a life insurance policy large enough to keep your partner out of debt if you were to pass;

for instance, if you hold a mortgage together, you don't want your spouse/partner to have to drain your savings due to the loss of your income. "Enough" is going to look like a much larger amount if you have young children, like David and Sarah do, or other dependents.

A *general* rule of thumb in your early adult years is to secure a policy that provides seven to ten times your salary, for the duration of time where that income would be necessary. Think about it as covering the mortgage, other debt, getting your children raised (for instance, if your spouse/partner dies you may need a nanny or additional help), and getting children through college, while still allowing you to save/have funds for retirement. Perhaps you aren't worried about covering the cost of college, but you do want to maintain a certain quality of life and still project future financial needs. Your financial advisor can help you determine what might be best for your particular family, in regards to the length of term and amount. The purpose is to cover the future financial needs so the surviving spouse/partner need not worry.

Although you might be able to get the lowest rate with a shorter policy—say, ten years—we recommend you take out a policy that will cover you for the entire length of time that your financial needs are high. Why? First of all, it would be easy to forget to buy a new ten-year policy if it's been ten years since you took out the first one. Secondly—and more importantly—term life insurance premiums will be much higher to purchase when you're forty than when you're thirty. This would be especially true if you were to have had any medical complications over the previous ten years that make you seem like a riskier candidate than when you bought your first policy. With life insurance, it's best to think *way* ahead into the future. We think it's best to lock in a decent rate for a term that reflects the duration of years you think your family would need support, should something happen to you.

Let's go back to David and Sarah. David decides that their income needs are likely to be the highest over the next twenty years, while their kids are still at home and getting through college. He decides to take out a twenty-year policy for $700,000. Or, perhaps he and Sarah have a thirty-year mortgage, and he wants a thirty-year policy to see that mortgage through; in that case, he might elect to take out a thirty-year policy for $1,000,000. Or a tiered approach could be taken, where David could buy a twenty-year $700,000 policy and a thirty-year $300,000 policy. That will give him a total of $1 million for twenty years while maintaining $300,000 of coverage for the remaining ten years of the need.

Thirty years into the future though, the story changes. David would be sixty-five and nearing retirement, if not retired already. Their expenses have lowered; maybe the mortgage is paid off, and their kids are through college and living on their own. At this point, David's human capital has diminished, but his financial capital has likely grown. If he were to pass away, Sarah would still have their retirement savings and any other investments to live on. At that point, the need for term insurance has diminished or gone away altogether.

PERMANENT INSURANCE

Let's say that, around age 60, David decides he wants to

pursue different insurance at that stage in life, for his legacy planning — something that might fall under the category of "permanent insurance." Permanent insurance is a broad term which describes life insurance policies that are guaranteed to provide a death benefit for your lifetime.

Note that you can pursue permanent insurance at any age you prefer; we're not implying you *have* to wait until you are in your 60s to pursue permanent insurance, like David. In fact, if you think you might want to purchase permanent insurance, it's most cost effective to set it up before you've acquired a list of medical ailments. However, it is most common to start with term and move on to permanent later in life because of the affordability factor, as well as change in needs and desires.

The two main types of permanent insurance are whole life and universal life. A **whole life insurance policy covers you typically until age 100 or 105 — theoretically, for your whole life**, hence the name. Because these policies are almost sure to be paid out, the premiums are much higher from the get-go. You're essentially buying the Cadillac of life insurance, and you'll be committed to pay those premiums for — once again — your whole life. It's possible that eventually, the dividends from the whole life investments will grow and help cover the premiums; however, it's important to remember that, whether or not those dividends help cover the cost, you're committed to pay the premiums throughout the duration of your life. Whole life insurance is mainly a **legacy planning tool**.

Term insurance and a permanent insurance plan, like whole life, can be layered. You might recognize that you want to start a whole life policy before you get much older or become ill, at which point the premiums would jump. If you determine that a whole life policy makes financial sense for you, then you can opt to layer on the permanent insurance toward the end of your term insurance plan or replace the term altogether.

Keep in mind though, that it's possible to be *over* insured — and that sets you up for missed opportunity cost. Make sure to evaluate all your financial goals (emergency, cash flow, retirement, college) with your insurance funding so you're not missing opportunities to pursue other investments.

Permanent insurance is an excellent tool for those who like the idea of leaving each child and/or grandchild an inheritance. Whole life does have an additional interesting, and perhaps useful, twist. It has a savings account component from which you may borrow (you will have to pay interest though).

However, for people who don't want to use it for a legacy planning tool, permanent insurance may not make sense. A permanent insurance policy commits you to pay large premiums during a season of life when you might have many other financial goals. If you were to unexpectedly lose your job or experience financial hardship, you could be stuck with those premium payments. At that point, you may have to either lower your death benefit amount, or drop the policy altogether. As with any investment, your decision to invest in permanent insurance should be determined by what you want to accomplish with that particular tool.

Other permanent insurance types are **universal life, vari-**

able **universal life, variable life,** and **survivorship.** Here are a few notes on each:

- Universal offers flexibility in your premiums and has a cash value component. As your life changes you have options; for instance, you may decide to maximize your premium payments in the early years, covering the current cost of insurance and also building up cash value. You could lower that payment to just the current cost of insurance when times are tight.
- Variable allows you to invest the cash value of your insurance policy in the stock market via what are called sub-accounts (mutual fund-like vehicles). In many cases, the dividends and growth from those investments can help assist in paying the insurance premiums. However those investments can go down as well, so it is truly variable and carries a risk.
- Variable Universal—you guessed it—combines the features of both variable and universal.
- Survivorship, what used to be known as "second-to-die" insurance, is a policy on two people, typically a married couple. It does not pay out until the second person dies.

Whether you are looking at term insurance or any of these permanent insurance policies, it is important you always understand all the intricacies of how the policy works and the pros and cons of your policy so you are comfortable with what you own.

OTHER TYPES OF INSURANCE

Most people are familiar with homeowner's insurance, car insurance, medical insurance, and so on. We're not going to get into those more familiar insurance types here. However, we do want to acquaint you with two other types of insurance (completely unrelated to each other) that are less well known, but might be worth investing in.

Long-term care insurance can be important if you anticipate expenses related to—you guessed it—long-term care. Multiple years in a nursing home can be a substantial cost, and this type of insurance can help cover those expenses. This type of insurance policy would be even more useful for someone with high medical needs, like an Alzheimer's or Parkinson's patient, who will likely need specialty care for a number of years. There are a few types of insurance policies (traditional long-term care, life insurance with long-term care, or annuity with long-term care) to fund such a risk. You would want to seek assistance vetting these appropriately to make sure you get the right policy for your situation.

Also, a **Personal Liability Umbrella Policy (PLUP)** can be an important tool to help protect you and your assets in the case of a lawsuit. A PLUP goes beyond the coverage you might already receive through your homeowner's insurance or car insurance.

Here are two scenarios when a PLUP would be valuable.

- Your regular delivery person notices that all of your packages are addressed to "Dr." One day, he stumbles on a loose board on your front steps and ends up breaking his neck. Assuming that you're wealthy, he decides to sue you for the full amount of his medical bills, along with additional costs related to emotional trauma and lost work time. The liability goes beyond what your homeowner's insurance would cover; however, a PLUP could provide the additional coverage needed.

- You get into a car accident with another uninsured car carrying five people. Who's going to pay those medical bills? The costs of extensive medical treatment can skyrocket. A PLUP would help cover the costs that go beyond what your car insurance covers. This can be particularly important if you're perceived as someone with great wealth, who might be seen as a prime target to sue. A PLUP can help you protect the wealth you've worked hard to build from evaporating, due to a random accident.

When considering how you might want to invest in insurance, consider what you mainly need insurance *for*. Primarily, insurance is a tool for your protection and, secondly, an estate planning tool. Generally, we don't recommend using insurance as an investment tool, unless you thoroughly understand all the complexities related to using insurance in a less traditional manner.

DEBT

Capitalism gave us a blessing and a curse when it gave us debt. In the capitalist system, a business owner has the mobility and flexibility to invest in a business *before* having the financial capital to do so. Taking out a loan can enable you to procure liquid cash when your assets are all tied up in illiquid holdings. In that way, debt can be a gift to entrepreneurs—the spark that enables them to move into a new building for their growing business, while they're dumping every last cent of their profits into current production. In other words, debt can be an integral tool for investment and growth.

Debt's investment possibilities are not limited to entrepreneurs. Teach your children and grandchildren to consider these other "investment" strategies with debt:

- Taking out student loans can be an investment in your human capital.
- Mortgage loans enable you to buy a house and start building up home equity.
- Debt can be a tax management strategy. For instance, let's say you want to buy a rental property before you have the cash ready, or buy your new home before you sell your old home. You might get a collateralized line of credit on your investment account, which would prevent you from being forced to draw a large sum from your IRA or take capital gains and have to pay income tax or capital gains tax on those funds when it is only for a temporary basis.
- Even credit card debt can help you build a good credit score, provided you pay your card off fully every month. Having good credit is a critical component of being able to get a loan, for either a business or a mortgage.
- Wise use of debt allows you to use money you don't have to build wealth and accelerate returns. For instance, let's say you take out a mortgage loan to buy a $400,000 rental property and put 20 percent down ($80,000). Your renter pays all expenses associated with the property (mortgage, taxes, insurance, etc.) In a year, you sell the property and it's gained 3 percent equity; you sell for $412,000. You've made a profit of $12,000, which is roughly 15 percent of the original amount of $80,000 you put down. That's a

great return on your investment! However, it's important to note that debt can magnify either positive *or* negative returns. For example, if the home had depreciated in value and you sold for $378,000, you would experience a loss on your investment of approximately $22,000 or 27.5 percent of your original $80,000 investment.

This brings us to an important point: there's a curse side to debt, too. If you don't handle debt responsibly, two consequences kick in, both of which can seriously cripple your financial future:

1. You get on the wrong side of compound interest.
2. You destroy your credit.

Let's talk more specifically about both.

DANGEROUS DEBT

We've already discussed the incredible power of compound interest when used in your favor, in long-term investments. Unfortunately, compounding interest can be just as powerful in its destructive capabilities when you pile up debt at high interest rates.

When Roger was in college, he observed several friends fund their lifestyles via credit cards. When they maxed out one card, they rolled the debt over onto another card. By the time they graduated, they owed thousands of dollars at high interest rates—not to mention what they already owed on student loans. They began their professional careers seriously burdened by the weight of that debt and haunted by their terrible credit rating.

A bad credit rating is not only dangerous financially but can also lead you to make decisions that are not in line with your values. For instance, you might be forced to take a lucrative job that you know will require long hours and huge stress, because of the weight of your debt. We know of a young man who graduated medical school with the desire to work with non-profits. However, because he had such staggering debt, he had to pursue a job at a for-profit hospital which drained him in every way.

Here's advice to pass on to your children and grandchildren: if you want to do much of anything as an adult—buy a new car at a good rate, get a mortgage loan, start up a business—you *need* good credit. You build up your good credit through responsible financial behavior. Pay off your credit card every month and pay your bills on time. Banks will choose to lend to you (or not) based on your previous behaviors, and how responsibly you've handled your finances. If you do a solid job building up good credit, you're going to have access to investment opportunities that you wouldn't have otherwise. That good credit score gives you leverage in the world.

If you wind up with a bad credit score, those opportunities can be denied you. You may find yourself unable to get a loan for a house or start-up business. Worst of all, the debt responsible for bringing down your score might get you on the wrong side of compounding interest.

Credit card debt works *against* you in the realm of compound interest. If you only pay off the minimum monthly payment on credit cards, your total debt could quickly grow at a compounding rate. Some people aren't trained to pay off their credit card each month. They like earning points, and having all the advertised benefits of the credit cards—they assume that if they can meet the minimum payment required, they're fine. But that's a losing strategy.

Credit cards may be useful, but unless you pay off the balance *in full* every month, the credit card companies end up earning much more from you than they ever plan to give back. If you don't pay off the balance, that 8, 9, 10, 17 percent interest is going to compound, and compound, and compound. People can easily fall into a vicious cycle where the debt can't be chased down.

Debt: The 28/36 Rule

One way you can teach your kids to stay in the good graces of the credit score raters is by teaching them the 28/36 percent rule:

- **Your housing expenses should not exceed 28 percent of your gross monthly income.**
- **Your total monthly debt payments should not exceed 36 percent of your gross monthly income.**

Here's an example of the **28 percent rule**: if you're earning a gross of $7,850 per month, you could have a housing expense of $2,200 per month: $7,850 x 0.28 = $2,200.

Mortgage lenders are not necessarily incentivized to help you maintain a rational mortgage amount. For example, just because you make $500,000 per year doesn't mean you *need* to spend $11,666 a month ([$500,000 x 0.28] ÷ 12 = $11,666) on your housing expense. Establish a reasonable housing expense and use the excess to save and invest for other goals. Choosing a large housing expense that stretches you to your maximum capacity will seriously impede your ability to put money toward other financial goals and if anything changes with your income or job, it could become a problem.

Now, let's stick with that same monthly income of $7,850, and apply the **36 rule**: $7,850 x 0.36 = $2,826. For a person making this income, with a $2,200 housing expense payment, their remaining debt from other loans should not exceed about $630. That would include credit card debt, monthly student loan payments, car loan payments, and so on. If you know those costs are substantial for you, then you would ideally commit to a housing expense that was even lower than 28 percent of your monthly gross income. The 28/36 rule is meant to be viewed as a *limit*, not as a target.

This rule will help you live within your means and help you handle your finances in a way that credit raters view as responsible. Rather than missing housing expense payments or other debt payments that are too high and seeing your credit score drop, you'll be getting gold stars for making payments on time and your score will rise.

Student Loans

Student loans can be an amazing investment: they can help people pursue higher education, which in turn, can lead to better jobs and higher income down the road. But does that mean it's advisable to take out as many student loans as might be required to go to the Dream School? We would caution against that.

For many families, it's helpful to have a general rule to reference in these weighty considerations. Here's our recommendation: **your *total* college debt should not equal more than your first year's salary.** If a parent or guardian is on the hook for those loans, that person should not sign up for more debt than they can afford, according to the 28/36 percent rule.

We want to clarify: when choosing careers and schools, it's important to remember that money isn't everything. We hope that our own kids can be true to themselves when choosing their future path, and that they follow their dreams, regardless of what the take-home pay is. However, we also want to urge parents and kids to think hard about the financial challenge you may be committing to if you choose an expensive school, anticipate a modest future salary, and aren't in a strong position to pay off loans quickly. Either you, or your kids, could be painfully committed to paying off loans for years at the expense of pursuing other worthy goals.

TAXES

Taxes are dynamic; in other words, they're always changing. The tax code itself often changes, and your life situation changes often too. Let's consider how each changing element would impact your financial decisions.

When tax policy changes, it can make a huge impact on how you would make investment decisions. For instance, let's say that you are a high-income earner and pay high income tax. You buy a stock in January, and you sell it in June, holding it for less than one year. Your gain on the sale of that stock would be classified as a **short-term capital gain,** and it would be taxed at ordinary income tax rates, a *higher rate* than if you'd held onto the stock for more than a year, which would have classified it as a **long-term capital gain.** Under our current tax code, short-term capital gains are taxed at ordinary income rates (as high as 37 percent), whereas long term capital gains are taxed at 0, 15, or 20 percent. That's a huge difference, and understandably, that element of the tax code could have a major impact on when you decide to sell your stocks.

Wade even deeper into the fine print of the tax code, and the decisions get more complicated. For instance, there is an entirely different tax number on gold investments: 28 percent. Dividends can also be taxed differently whether they are considered qualified or nonqualified. And these are just a few of the details related to taxation on investments that need to be paid attention to. (This is one reason why we recommend recruiting a CPA as part of your "team" and have them work collaboratively with your financial advisor on strategies — see our recommendations in the Appendix.)

Taxes will also change with your different phases of life, as well. Let's say that you're over 65, and you're receiving health insurance through Medicare. Did you know that Medicare insurance premiums are means-based? The amount of capital gains you recognize, along with income from IRAs, pensions or interest, all gets factored into your Medicare premium cost, which is based on your Modified Adjusted Gross Income. The actions you take regarding your investments and income (and managing/mitigating with a collaborative team) will have an impact on something as seemingly unrelated as your health insurance.

Your stage of life may also determine what retirement account you should draw from first, whether it's an IRA or a joint account. Depending on whether or not you're receiving a pension, you may want to adjust the timing of when you start collecting Social Security. When the tax code meets your personal life, a lot of moving puzzle pieces are at play. You need to be mindful and tactical about your financial approach, so that you're in a better place to pass on your wealth.

By working with a CPA on your taxes along with your financial advisor on distribution and investment strategies, you can benefit from a team who will work together to help you feel more in control about your tax obligations. Left to your own devices, you may neglect to consider the impact taxes could have on your financial picture. Do not underestimate the impact that your tax strategy can have on your quality of life, and the size of your inheritance. The rate of return for making good tax decisions can be as impactful as investment returns.

We're not trying to stiff the government in issuing this advice; we're simply trying to point out that there are many different factors at play when you're dealing with taxes. Unintended consequences can occur if you're not mindful of how your financial decisions may impact your tax obligation. We fully believe in contributing our fair share to the government through paying taxes. However, we also believe there's no need to be foolish in paying more than we're obligated to, simply because we ignored the details of the tax code.

THE VALUE OF STRESS TESTING

In these four major areas of your finances, we can't recommend one tool highly enough: stress testing. **Stress testing is a way to evaluate different possible scenarios that may come about in the future, and how those scenarios may impact your finances.** For instance, what would your financial picture look like if you retired at age 62, rather than at age 65? Or, how would your financial picture change if you decide to buy a vacation home? These sorts of hypothetical questions come up all the time when people are making big decisions related to investments, insurance, debt, and taxes—which makes stress testing an especially valuable step in your decision-making process.

The concept of stress testing is likely familiar to anyone with an engineering background, similar to Roger. When new products are developed or old products are revised, engineers are often tasked with ensuring the end product will perform within the specifications. Have you ever seen the crash test commercials on TV where a car is hurled into a wall and the test dummy is violently thrown around? That is stress testing. Did the air bag deploy? Did the front end collapse like an accordion to absorb the impact? Was the test dummy unscathed? This is what we advocate you do with your financial plans on a periodic basis.

The process used for stress testing should be designed to focus on addressing any gaps or opportunities in the following key areas:

- Tax Efficiency: Are my distributions, investment holdings, estate plan, types of accounts, etc., optimized for my specific situation and current circumstances?

- Wealth Transfer: Will my assets go where I want them to if something were to happen to me? Who will control the assets? Have my wishes changed since originally establishing?
- Charitable Impact: Based on current laws and my personal desires, am I employing the best strategy for charitable giving?

In other words, stress testing helps you evaluate whether or not your current financial strategies and products are accomplishing your family's key goals and objectives. The process helps you identify opportunities that you may have overlooked which could improve your outcome.

Think about your own life. It's likely you can track many different stages and phases that have occurred over time as your family and financial dynamics shifted. Some of these stages are obvious, like retirement, marriage, or having a child. However, other stages are less predictable, like the timing of an inheritance or an illness. In any case, when a major event or life change occurs, your current plan can become obsolete. Ask yourself: does your current plan account for the most recent changes and your desire for the future?

By going through the process of stress testing, you're able to look at many of the "what-ifs" of your future and consider the range of possible outcomes for each possible scenario so that you can ideally aim yourself toward the best one. Think of it as standing at the intersection of your financial and emotional decisions and determining the best route possible to effectively accomplish your goals. Stress testing will help you optimize your financial picture in each of the four areas we've discussed in this chapter.

CHECK THE FRIDGE: REVIEW YOUR FINANCIAL PICTURE

Imagine opening the door to your fridge. You might see some produce, some condiments, some leftovers. Perhaps there are a few meals in the freezer. That fridge is going to look different during each stage of life—as a young single person, the fridge might only contain a few things. It might be bursting when you have kids running around with robust appetites. It might reflect certain dietary preferences when you get older. If you plan to host a dinner party, the fridge's contents will look different—you'll buy some new special ingredients, or clean out some older items to make more room.

The fridge says something about where you're at in life and how you're providing for the people in your care. When you buy new groceries, you need to regularly evaluate what needs go to into the fridge. Periodically, you'll go through it and see what's expired to clean it out.

In the same way, your financial picture is going to constantly change. Your needs will change; your goals will change. As it does, you're going to want to check the fridge. See what needs to go in; see what's expired and should come out. Regularly revisit your financial picture to make sure it's still working for you. Stress test your financial plans regularly—and pay particular attention to the four areas that have been discussed in this chapter.

Investment, insurance, debt, and taxes: these four topics may seem dissimilar, but, when handled well, all of them can still be viewed as investment strategies. Insurance can help build your estate; smart tax maneuvers can help protect and build your investments; taking out loans at the right time, for the right reason can help build your equity; and making smart tax decisions can result in great rates of return.

Alternately, all of them can drain your estate if you're not mindful about your approach. Many of these topics can be complex, which is one reason why you might find it helpful to work with a team of professionals, not only to evaluate your current scenario for gaps and issues, but also for opportunities and ensuring you are building the best financial life possible. We have tried to provide enough baseline financial literacy in this chapter to equip you to seek out deeper knowledge on your own, should you want to explore any topic in more depth.

PART THREE

PLANNING YOUR LEGACY AND PROTECTING YOUR FAMILY

Organize important information via a Personal Wealth Organizer so that it's easy for your family to find and review. Acquaint yourself with legal tools that may be useful in your estate planning. Finally, make yourself aware of potentially dangerous biases, behaviors, and circumstances that could undermine your efforts to pass it on.

CHAPTER SIX

YOUR LEGACY PLAN
AND LEGAL TOOLS

"A goal without a plan is just a wish."

ANTOINE DE SAINT-EXUPÉRY

Around fifteen years ago, a client came into our office with a garbage bag full of random bits of information which were all related to her recently passed mother's finances. There were stock certificates, and statements, and other bits of paper— some of which were relevant, and some of which weren't.

With a sigh, the daughter told us that she had thought she'd already settled all of the financial details of her mother's estate, but after coming across more paperwork, she'd realized that her mother held other assets she still needed to deal with. It was clear she was feeling tired, stressed, and reluctant to return to logistical hassles related to an experience as painful as her mother's death. Our interaction with her made us realize how desperately our clients needed help in setting up the details of their estate—not just for their sakes, but for the sake of their children.

Although we see ourselves primarily as financial planners and investment managers, this instance made us realize that one of the biggest gifts we can give to families is *organization*. It's enormously difficult—not to mention emotionally heartrending—for adult children to have to sleuth out their parents' financial details after their passing. One of the best acts you can take in providing for your children is to provide your *details*—in an organized, collected format.

This chapter is going to detail what, exactly, needs to be organized as you prepare your estate and legacy plan. We're also going to discuss important points to consider when legacy planning, and we'll discuss some helpful legal tools.

Let's get honest for a second: we know that people hate thinking about the kind of considerations we're going to cover in this chapter. Going through the various steps of estate planning seems about as fun as cleaning out your basement. But remember, the people who end up bearing the brunt of your failure to plan are your *children*.

If you've read this far in the book, you obviously care enough about your kids to want to pass on your wealth and values. If you care that much, then we encourage you to do the hard work required to plan your legacy as well. Choosing to do so means you're choosing to protect them during one of the most potentially vulnerable times of their lives: when they lose you.

DON'T WAIT

If you're older, you may know already that estate planning is a topic you need to deal with. However, if you're in a stage of life like us, with young kids running around, you might be tempted to conclude that "estate planning" is something you can put off for a long time still.

In reality, having young kids at home is one of the most important seasons of life to establish an estate plan. Establishing a trustee and a guardian for your children is *crucial* for you to do while you still have young children. We've included a substantial section on how to go about selecting these key people in our Appendix. If you still have kids in your home, we recommend you turn to that section immediately and identify people to fulfill those roles as soon as possible.

Likewise, a family with young children can become extremely vulnerable if there's no life insurance set up or no trust established to avoid the dangerous circumstance of sudden wealth. (We'll discuss that more in our next chapter).

When there's no written estate plan established, the courts have to figure out the plan for you based on state law and sometimes discretion. That means thousands of dollars sucked up in legal fees, additional time, and potentially a much different outcome than intended.

Beneficiaries of an estate—i.e., the people you love—will have to pay anywhere from 3 to 8 percent of their inheritance on legal probate fees *if there's no will or trust*.[31] It will also take far longer for the estate to be distributed—as long as a year or more.

---

31 Probate is the court-supervised process of authenticating a last will and testament, or distributing an estate when there is no documented plan.

The courts may not make decisions that reflect your wishes either. When your money hits that system, the courts will primarily consider your family tree, and look for your next of kin. Your estate will likely be assigned to those closest relatives. But what if that next of kin was a terrible person to you, and you never wanted that person to have your money? What if your next of kin struggles with drug addiction, and shouldn't be trusted with a large sum of money? If you want your estate to go to the people you trust and love the most, you need to clarify those names ahead of time.

Depending on the size of your estate and the state you live in, you're also likely to give a disproportionate amount of your estate to the government in taxes if you haven't proactively figured out a strategy for transferring assets to beneficiaries efficiently and effectively. The bigger the estate, the greater potential impact of tax owed. To not have a prepared, formalized, proactive, and thoughtful estate plan is to let the government decide where your money goes.

With more tangible assets, the scenarios can get even more confusing. The stress level and potential for family conflict may also ratchet up. Who gets the house? Who gets Dad's vintage convertible? What about the family farm? If the inheritance is illiquid and tied up, like in the case of a family farm, your children are going to have to figure out what they're going to do with it. What if one sibling wants to sell, and two want to keep it? What if bills start coming in, but there's no liquid cash to pay off creditors? If there's no clear estate plan in place, then pain, confusion, and family conflict is worsened.

Here's the point: **failing to plan *is* a de facto plan.** It means you let the courts and the government decide what to do with your money. It also means you may invite unnecessary conflict into your family. However, when you make a clear, well-organized estate plan, you are not only able to clearly identify your beneficiaries, you can also clarify your wishes for what should be done with your assets.

We understand the temptation to put it off. Famous celebrities like Prince, Sonny Bono, and Aretha Franklin all died without an estate plan in place. However, even though failing to plan is easy for you, it creates a great big mess for everyone else. Particularly if you're known as a person with wealth, like many of those celebrities, there's a high likelihood that people will come out of the woodwork and try to make a claim on your estate.

In summary: don't wait to take the steps we're going to recommend in this chapter. There's too much at stake to risk putting it off.

IDENTIFYING YOUR BENEFICIARIES

As you consider the various legal tools and provisions related to your legacy which we'll discuss in this chapter, you might be thinking of each one in the context of your family. The names of your loved ones might mentally be assigned to different roles, or assets. We want to address some important factors related to that thought of beneficiaries before we get into anything else.

First: it is just as important for you to identify a **contingent beneficiary** (a backup beneficiary), as it is to identify your primary beneficiary. For example, many people choose their spouse as their beneficiary, but what if you and your spouse die on the same flight? With no contingent beneficiary named, the court will decide where your money goes, instead of you.

Secondly, we highly recommend that you **thoughtfully consider how your estate plan will impact your beneficiaries**, so that you can make sure you're helping them, not complicating their financial situation. This can be especially important when dealing with taxes. Here are a few examples of how people's lives could be unhelpfully disrupted by an abrupt change in their financial scenario:

- You might have a special needs daughter who participates in a number of programs that are provided through the government. It's possible that she might lose access to some of her familiar providers or programs if her financial situation were to dramatically change.
- You have a son who works as a venture capitalist who's paying 37 percent income tax and has more money than he knows what to do with. It makes little sense to name him as the primary beneficiary on your IRA, which will be fully income taxed at the highest rate when he withdraws it. It might make more sense to direct that money into an inheritance for your grandchildren or charity.
- If your child is in a troubled marriage and is considering divorce, a sudden inheritance could seriously complicate those divorce proceedings and majorly increase stress.

In certain instances, what you consider to be helpful might actually hinder or disrupt someone's life. When identifying your beneficiaries, be considerate of the people around you. Think about who they are, how they use their money, and where they are in life. As much as possible, be considerate of how your inheritance could have the most positive impact on your beneficiaries' lives so that you can bless them.

KEEP YOUR PLAN CURRENT

It's also important to understand that you need to review your plan often, especially during times of life including marriage or childbirth, when new people enter the family photos — or, tragically, when some leave it during times of death or divorce.

Revisit your named beneficiaries and consider: Is anyone missing? Should any names be changed? Your feelings about one family member may be totally different in five years. A beneficiary may predecease you. Your children's financial needs may radically alter from what they are now, in several more years. For all these reasons, the estate plan needs to be revisited. **We recommend reviewing your estate plan at least every three to five years, or when you know of a change in people, laws or a significant variance in assets.**

Aside from the personal reasons you might want to update your plan, it's also important to pay attention to changing tax code or estate and gift tax rules. New presidents bring new administrations with new policies. Any number of federal laws related to estate planning can change. As you collect more assets, and build more wealth, it's crucial to keep an eye on the tax ramifications of increased wealth.

When one family originally set up their estate plan, for example, they were operating with a federal estate tax exemption of $675,000. In other words, each parent was only allowed to give a gift of up to $675,000 to their beneficiaries before the government taxed the rest (up to 55 percent at that time). The parents developed an elaborate plan so that they could give more than that amount to their kids before incurring tax. They developed a family trust and survivors' trust, an irrevocable life insurance trust, and a charitable lead trust.

Fast forward eighteen years: the matriarch of this family is still healthy, and the federal estate tax exemption has now increased to $11.58 million per person. Many of the complicated tools the family put in place are now irrelevant, for estate tax avoidance purposes. Estate plans like this need to be regularly updated, to suit the changing laws or ensure the family still has other purposes in mind with what they have designed, aside from estate tax mitigation.

Simply put: estate planning cannot be a one-time task. Although policy changes might favor you one day, they may not favor you the next.

Estate planning might feel as "fun" as cleaning out the basement—however, we're going to do our best to give you steps to ease the process. First, you can simplify the process by putting it in a step-by-step format; we're going to tell you how. Second, identify your people: your attorney, executor, guardians, and trustees as needed. The result will be a clear, well organized, detailed gift to your family.

Let's go over each step in greater depth.

THE PERSONAL WEALTH ORGANIZER

The woman we described at the beginning of this chapter came in with a big bag full of random bits of paper related to her mother's accounts. Our improvement? A big, black binder full of organized bits of paper, related to *all* necessary details of her financial and legal life. We call it the Personal Wealth Organizer, and it's meant to be a one-stop-shop for your family members with all the information they might need in settling your legacy or in the event you are incapacitated.

Here are some of the areas where we have clients collect information:

1. *Professional Advisors and Key Service Providers:* Provide a list of the names and contact information of all key players related to handling your affairs. Some obvious candidates would be your financial advisor, estate planning attorney, CPA, and insurance representatives. You could also include the names of other important people who were integral to the running of your affairs—a personal assistant, for instance, or your property manager. We list all of these professionals first in the binder, because they're often incredibly helpful to surviving family members in going through the rest of the binder.

2. *Most Recent Investment Review:* This would help a beneficiary or power of attorney know how the portfolio is allocated, making it easier to work with a financial advisor on where best to pull funds needed to pay bills, pay funeral costs, or understand the type of assets to be distributed at death.

3. *Bank, Brokerage, and Retirement Accounts:* Provide the statements for your bank, brokerage, and retirement

accounts. The account numbers, titles and beneficiaries should be laid out on the cover page. Remember to make sure that every account with an ability to name a beneficiary has a primary beneficiary *and* a contingent beneficiary. If you and your primary beneficiary pass away in the same accident, ensure you have someone next on the list to receive the assets.

4. *Liabilities:* Provide a comprehensive list of your debts and creditors, such as your mortgage information or other business liabilities.

5. *Financial Plan:* This is a document that brings together all your financial affairs—investments, pensions, Social Security, long-term care, life insurance, expenses, etc.— and would assist your health and financial power of attorneys on understanding the entire picture of cash flow, tax bracket, IRA required minimum distributions, etc.

6. *Custodian, Trustee and/or Guardianship Appointments:* Clearly list any accounts that you are custodian, trustee, or guardian on because if something has changed with your health then they need to be aware you can no longer serve on their accounts and make appropriate adjustments.

7. *Estate Plan:* Provide a copy of your current estate plan (a "core" estate plan will include a will, revocable trust, healthcare proxy, durable power of attorney, and any other HIPAA or living will documents you've put together) so your executor can begin to know the steps and process. Clearly list where the original is located, as well, because they will need that in order to move forward on the estate distributions process. We also include this because the binder is a resource to help you ensure you've crossed every "t," and dotted every "i." For the

next five, ten, and twenty years, you have quick, easy access to review your estate plan for appropriate changes.

8. *Insurance:* Provide statements for all your insurance policies, such as life, disability, long-term care, personal liability umbrella policy, auto, homeowner, and healthcare. You should also provide beneficiary details on the life insurance, as well as a recap of general benefits and premiums for the life insurance and long-term care so you can ensure accuracy. This will also help you quickly review the policies in the future for any changes that should be made.

9. *Pension Plan and Social Security Statements:* We include these in the binder to remind the beneficiary/beneficiaries to notify these institutions for the new calculation of benefits (i.e., widow benefits or survivor benefits).

10. *Biographical Information:* This section directs people to note where certain key documents can be located (both the original and a copy), such as your birth certificate, Social Security card, driver's license, passport, marriage certificate, children's birth certificates, and other important documents that your family may need.

11. *Miscellaneous:* Under "Miscellaneous," we cover some of the other important areas of information, which don't neatly fall into their own category: deeds, titles, safe deposit box information, P.O. Box/storage unit information, and so on. In each section, we direct people to write down all details needed to help family members locate and access each item. Then, we direct people to record other important information: important employment/ military service/rental information; a list of collectibles with details about location and storage; pet information, including the name of your veterinarian; credit card providers; a list of bills that are paid via automatic

payment online; and any other miscellaneous details that might be relevant. This may sound like overkill, however bill paying (for the power of attorney or executor) can be one of the most confusing and stressful points; not knowing what is automatic versus snail mail or electronic can be a cumbersome task to sort through.

12. *Passwords and Usernames:* Your family will also need a list of passwords to access your online accounts, so that they can contact people and take steps as needed. You may consider using a password app—an app that uses one password to hold all passwords—or take another route.

It's a lot, isn't it? It didn't used to be so comprehensive. We used to simply encourage people to organize the details of their estate. However, our advice was only getting people so far. Inevitably, people forgot to provide certain details that their families would need. Eventually, we determined we could have the most impact on clients' lives if we created this wealth organizer *for* them.

Except for highly motivated people, assembling all this information independently can feel overwhelming. We came to the conclusion that we had to provide this as a gift to clients and assemble (at least 90 percent of it) for them and work collaboratively to assemble the rest.

In book format, we're unfortunately not able to provide the personal hand-holding that can be so important in assembling the Personal Wealth Organizer. However, we do want to encourage you to enlist the help of your financial advisor and/or your estate attorney. Having accountability and encouragement can be incredibly helpful in getting this large project done.

The binder is also an incredible tool for clients because it helps clarify where there might be gaps in their overall plan. When we go through the process of completing the Personal Wealth Organizer and gather everything in one place, it becomes easier to spot where there may be issues that should be addressed or if there are opportunities that are not being utilized. As a result, our clients have peace of mind, knowing they have the most optimal and up-to-date financial and legal plan in place. In that way, the Personal Wealth Organizer is just as much a gift for you in organizing your current financial affairs, as it is a gift of organization to your children.

THE PERSONAL WEALTH ORGANIZER: AN EXCUSE TO COMMUNICATE

Many people feel reluctant to talk about their estate plan with their children. Let's be honest: it's an awkward topic! If you don't feel like you can talk about these emotional issues, let the Personal Wealth Organizer be an excuse to kickstart a conversation. When you assemble your binder, you're required to dig up information from many different areas of your life, some of which touch on your kids' lives. Use those points of connection to let them know what you're doing, and why. From there, you could set up a time to talk with your family members about some of the details of your estate plan that will affect them.

Here are some signs your family might be ready to have these estate planning conversations, as noted in *Creating the Good Will*, by Elizabeth Arnold[32]:

---

32 Arnold, Elizabeth. *Creating the Good Will: The Most Comprehensive Guide to Both the Financial and Emotional Sides of Passing on Your Legacy.* New York: Portfolio, 2007.

- Jokes are made at holiday gatherings about who will get what. "I want the china!" Or, "I don't care about dishes, so long as I get Mom's engagement ring."
- Intergenerational conversations often include put-down remarks, like, "Mom, you're getting so forgetful."
- Family members don't get along with each other, to the point that they avoid spending time together.
- There's gossip about how certain members of the family don't handle money well or take poor care of their belongings.
- There are comparison conversations among family members, arguing over who is loved most. For example, "Grandpa paid for all my soccer expenses because I'm his favorite grandchild."

Pay attention to the extremes in communication too: if your family *never* talks about what might happen when Grandma dies, or *only* talks about what happens when she passes—those could be signs you need to initiate a family talk about your inheritance as well.

As financial advisors, we often end up being part of those conversations. Sometimes, we're the excuse that our clients use to start them! We encourage our clients to say, "My financial advisor recommended we talk about my legacy plan." Consider whether or not it might feel helpful to have one of your professional advisors be part of the conversation with you and your family members, as a mediator or a guide.

The table of contents alone in the Personal Wealth Organizer can often help your kids realize the importance of a conversation and, ultimately, of having had collected information. You can ask them, "If something were to happen to us tomorrow, would you know where to find our account information? Or our online passwords? Do you know who our most important advisors are?" The honest answer from most children would be that they have no idea. Most family members realize quickly what a help the Personal Wealth Organizer will be. You may be at a stage where you only want to share where the Organizer is located, or you may be ready to divulge all asset information. The point is: you start and it can evolve from there.

We usually pull about 90 percent of the organizer together for our clients. Obviously, there are certain things we can't do; we don't know where every client keeps their birth certificate, or the bank lock box number and location. However, the more that we do pull together, the more we feel like we're giving back a needed service to our clients' spouses and kids.

If you feel confident putting together your own Personal Wealth Organizer, we encourage you to do so. If it feels too overwhelming, there are many professionals who can help you along the way.

LEGAL TOOLS

There are a number of legal tools which can provide important clarity for your family members after you pass, which will help ensure your legacy is carried out in the way you want. In fact—there are so many legal tools to use with financial planning, we could probably write a lengthy book just on that topic! However, that's not our purpose here.

Our goal here is to give you *enough* information about

some especially useful tools so that you will feel more equipped when you sit down with your attorney to map out the best strategy for your family. By acquainting you with the basics and purpose of some of the tools out there, we're hoping to provide a launch pad for you to seek out further information as will benefit your particular situation.

Your estate planning attorney will have more expertise with each legal tool, and can answer the specific questions you might have about using the tool for your own situation. Let's look at several of these tools more closely.

WILLS AND REVOCABLE LIVING TRUSTS

When helping our clients create their estate plans, we recommend they review the benefits of establishing a revocable living trust versus a will so they may determine what is best for their family. **The trust provides detailed, confidential, time-stamped specifications on the assets which go to beneficiaries.** In other words, if you want your children to receive their inheritance in steady payments stretched out over a number of years, that's something a revocable living trust can accomplish. The trust won't become public, which means all your requests will be kept private.

Even for people who have set up a trust, you should still create a simple will to clarify what should happen with any items that were not retitled to the trust or do not have a contractual beneficiary. The will also governs additional matters such as guardians, tangible personal property (Susan gets Dad's guitar; Matt gets Dad's tools, etc.), your forgiveness of any debts owed to you, and so on. One type of simple will is a "pour-over" will. **A pour-over will ensures that** any assets which weren't retitled as part of your trust during your life will still be "poured over" into the trust at death. It essentially serves as a "catch all."

There are many ways to personalize and set restrictions in revocable living trusts. For example, you might develop an estate plan that distributes 25 percent of your assets to your kids outright and keeps the rest in a restricted trust. You could change the percentage of what they receive outright, according to your beneficiaries' ages. At age thirty, they might receive 30 percent. At age fifty, they might receive the whole. Restrictions like these would, presumably, give your children more autonomy with their inheritance as they mature and have a shorter time span over which they need to stretch the money.

The available tools provided by a trust can also help if you feel any concern about your children potentially getting divorced. By employing particular restrictions and wording for asset protection, you can add a layer of protection to guard your children's assets from potential divorce, creditors, or malpractice.

Think of a **will** and a **revocable living trust** as two tools which stand side by side, but work together. Both are drafted by an attorney, and both provide specifications about what should happen to your assets after you die. However, a trust allows for more levers and stipulations over how those assets are given out. A trust allows more flexibility around how money is managed and distributed over time.

One important difference to understand between a will

and a trust: **a will becomes public information, whereas a trust is handled privately.** A will goes through the probate system and is handled by the courts. All the information in a will will eventually become public record.

Because a will tends to be simpler than a trust, it can often be less expensive to create on the front end. Since it may be cheaper and easier, some people only go so far as to create a will for their estate—and that is okay. If you are looking for added confidentiality and the specifications that a trust can provide, then establishing both a revocable living trust *and* a pour-over will would be advisable. Although setting up both will cost more up front to establish, the distribution costs are minimized later on, because you've already laid out your distribution plan with an attorney and it will not go through probate.

If you choose to set up a trust, then once you've completed that process, you'll be told to go "fund it." This is an important step; if none of your assets are in your trust title, it's not funded, and your family will have to go through the probate process in the courts. Failing to fund your trust is more common than you may think, which is why we feel it is an important point to mention. **To fund your trust, you need to change the title on your assets to the trust name.** You'll go to your bank, for example, and rename your joint account as a trust. Contact your brokerage firm and have them rename your joint account as a trust. Some attorneys even advise putting your house and cars as the title of the trust, although others advise differently.

Your attorney can help you determine what should be in the trust's name. After the assets have been renamed as a trust, that's still your money, and you get to handle it with the same freedom as if it were a normal joint bank account. The difference is that, when you die, your attorney and executor can process your estate distribution per your written wishes immediately (rather than having to go through the court system), and that will all be handled privately.

Whatever estate plan method you use, you're simplifying the process for your executor and beneficiaries down the road by doing the hard work now to get it right. That makes it worth the time on the front end. The best way to make things easy for your executor and beneficiaries is to title everything and name beneficiaries according to your estate plan. We see a lot of people develop estate plans, but then fail to carry that communication forward, or they're inconsistent about implementation. The more inconsistently you title your assets, the more room for error there is when your assets are in someone else's hands.

We recognize there are more stipulations and tools for estate planning than we've mentioned here; the process is not one-size-fits-all, nor is it black and white. Work with your estate attorney to discuss the steps that will make the most sense for your particular situation.

Accounts with Named Beneficiaries

It's important to know there are some accounts are not automatically controlled by your trust at death. Accounts with beneficiary designations, like your 401(k)s, IRAs, Roth IRAs, annuities, and life insurance are contractual agreements for which you have *named beneficiaries*; because of those contractual agreements, the beneficiary designation controls how the asset passes, not your will or revocable trust. 401(k)s will always be titled as 401(k)s. Your IRA will always be an IRA. No matter what your will or trust says, the *beneficiary form* is what matters when these assets are distributed. Put another way, the contractual agreements in IRAs, Roth IRAs, 401(k)s, annuities and insurance (i.e., the beneficiary designations you make), supersede anything in your will or trust.

That said, make sure you have the beneficiary you want designated! Imagine Andrea gets remarried and she remembers to change the beneficiary in her will to her new husband, Shane, but she forgets to change the named beneficiary on her IRA or 401(k), which is still in the name of her ex-husband, Chris. That money will go to Andrea's ex-husband, which is probably not what she'd prefer.

As you update your estate plan, get in the habit of checking your beneficiaries on your IRA, Roth IRA, 401(k), annuities, and life insurance as well to make sure they still reflect your wishes.

Charitable Trusts

Many people can think of charitable organizations that are close to their hearts which they want to benefit in their legacy as well. There are several other ways trusts can be beneficial, such as designating assets for charity.

Charitable Remainder Trusts are a broad category of trusts that can enable you to utilize an income stream from the trust while you are alive; then, when you die, your selected charity receives the remainder of the money you place in the trust. Not only are these tools a way to leave a legacy, but people typically put highly appreciated assets into them so they have immediate diversification with an income stream, and can manage the taxation. The two types of Charitable Remainder Trusts are:

- *Charitable remainder unitrust (CRUTs)*: The income stream you receive is based on the donated value, but is assessed each year and adjusts. At death, the charity receives the remainder.
- *Charitable remainder annuity trust (CRATs)*: The income stream you receive is based on the donated value and does not change. At death, the charity receives the remainder.

Charitable Lead Trusts work in the opposite fashion of a Charitable Remainder Trust. Your chosen charity receives an income stream for a set period of time (a fixed number of years, or while you're living), but when you die, your beneficiary receives the money.

There are additional ways you can designate charitable beneficiaries such as Donor Advised Funds, beneficiaries on IRAs, bequests, family foundations, etc., which can have additional tax advantages but those further specifics would be better to discuss, once again, with an estate planning attorney.

Charitable trusts can be a way to make a positive impact on society—and on your family. Giving has been a major theme of this book, and it's a powerful way that families can demonstrate their values to their children, even after death.

Irrevocable Life Insurance Trust

Another common legacy tool used by wealthy families is an **irrevocable life insurance trust (ILIT)**, which is mainly used to **avoid or limit taxes on your estate.** An ILIT is used to hold life insurance proceeds for your family outside of your estate. When money is put in an ILIT, it is no longer yours, hence the term "irrevocable." Now, why would you want to do that?

The federal government determines a limit to how much you can give your beneficiaries from your estate before it is taxed, called the Federal Estate Tax Exemption. In 2020, that limit is the highest it's ever been, at $11.58 million per person. If your estate falls *below* that government-established number, your estate won't be taxed. If it's *above* that number, your estate *will* be taxed. Here is an important consideration to keep in mind: life insurance death benefits are included in your estate tax calculation. Life insurance proceeds are not income taxable, but they are included in the estate tax calculation and could push the estate to go over that Federal Estate Tax Exemption limit.

Let's say your estate, when including your $4 million life insurance proceeds, totals $14 million, which means it's $2.42 million over the current Federal Estate Tax Exemption limit of $11.58 million. The limit has ranged over the years and is a bit of a moving target. You know that a new administration might bring new limits and your advisor has told you that current laws will revert that limit back to $5 million in 2026. You want to simplify your estate planning as much as you can to get around that moving target and still ensure you can leave your heirs the amount you desire.

If your goal is to pass on wealth and are concerned your

estate will be greater than the Federal Estate Tax Exemption, you can use this irrevocable life insurance trust strategy. To set it up, you would typically buy a permanent life insurance policy, often survivorship, inside your trust. In our example, a $4 million life insurance policy puts you $2.42 million over the $11.58 limit; that means $2.42 million would be subject to the estate tax rate (the top marginal rate being 40 percent—that's a lot). But if you put that insurance in an irrevocable life insurance trust, the $4 million is not counted toward your estate total and therefore not taxed at that high rate; you'd be left with the remaining $10 million estate, which is below the limit. In this way, an ILIT can be a useful planning tool for large estates.

Generation Skipping Trust

The last key asset transferring tool for wealthy families that we will mention here is planning for the Generation Skipping Transfer (GST) tax with a GST Trust. This planning tends to be utilized when the intent is for assets to benefit multiple generations, or when the second generation is already successful and wealthy in their own right. Rather than have assets transfer from the first generation to the second when the family knows that second generation is well above the Federal Estate Tax Limit and the inheritance will simply add to the pot to be taxed at the death of the second generation, they may utilize the GST Trust to move the funds to the third generation, therefore "skipping" the second generation. This can be designed to still allow income access for the second generation as well. The details of logistics and limitations can be reviewed by your estate planning attorney, however we wanted to at least bring the concept to light here.

OTHER IMPORTANT DOCUMENTS

We've said plenty about how your money will be distributed—but what about everything else? What about your funeral plans? What about your wishes for how your family members live out your legacy? And what if you—God forbid—end up with a condition that makes you incapacitated from making decisions related to your healthcare or quality of life?

There are some other essential documents that belong in your estate plan which are important for you, and even more important to your family. We'll start with the document made famous in the memorable case of Terri Schiavo: the living will.

Living Will

Terri Schiavo was in the prime of her life when she suffered an abrupt cardiac arrest. Although emergency workers were able to successfully resuscitate her, she had suffered so much brain damage due to the arrest, she remained in a coma. Ultimately, health workers changed her status to "persistent vegetative state."

After several years of no improvement, even after experimental nerve treatments, her husband and legal guardian, Michael, elected to remove the feeding tube which was keeping her alive. He argued that Terri wouldn't have wanted to live the rest of her life as a "vegetable." However, Terri's parents challenged his petition; they wanted Terri to be kept alive with continued artificial nutrition and hydration. They said that, as a Roman Catholic, Terri would have opposed the effective "euthanization" of removing the feeding tube.

A major battle over Terri's fate ensued, and the case became famous as it dragged through the courts.[33] Altogether, the family pursued fourteen different appeals, along with countless motions, petitions, and interventions. It became a politically polarizing issue, received direct involvement from then-President George W. Bush, and even reached the Supreme Court. Finally, Terri's feeding tube was removed. She passed away on March 31, 2005.

Terri Schiavo's story is a sad one that turned ugly, as her husband was pitted against her parents in a long, grisly legal battle. The money spent on legal fees and her healthcare costs are almost unimaginable. However, most of the cost and conflict in Terri's story would have been avoided with a living will.

A living will provides your family members with your desires for medical treatment if you cannot act. It is a legal document (sometimes included within your healthcare power of attorney) that has specific instructions about whether or not you want to be resuscitated and/or taken off life support, were you to end up in an irreversible vegetative state like Terri Schiavo. This living will could alleviate enormous stress, guilt, and confusion on the part of your family members, should this tragedy come to you.

Young people like Terri in their twenties, thirties and even forties, may believe they're invincible. No one thinks about becoming incapacitated, for example — an estate plan is seen as something for the elderly. However, as we've said before

---

33 Vance, J. D. "Remembering Terry Schiavo, Why You Need a Living Will." Vance Parker Law, PLLC, January 1, 2018. https://vparkerlaw.com/remembering-terry-schiavo/.

in this chapter—you'll be saving your family enormous heartache if you *don't wait* to complete a document like this. The harsh reality is that death or incapacity can happen at any time.

Power of Attorney: Healthcare and Durable

Because Terri Schiavo had not done any formal estate planning, she had also failed to identify either a healthcare power of attorney, or a durable power of attorney. Undoubtedly, not having these designees also contributed to the long, complicated legal case surrounding her life and death.

The healthcare power of attorney is the person who will confer with doctors and make decisions around your healthcare. That person should have the emotional strength and steadiness to make these loaded decisions. You should also consider the *location* of your healthcare power of attorney. There's a good chance your healthcare power of attorney might have to move among different hospitals and nursing homes to speak to medical professionals. Ideally, your healthcare power of attorney will have the proximity to do that easily, but it is not impossible for them to handle things from another state.

The durable/financial power of attorney deals with the financial side; they write the checks to pay your bills. This might be the same person you chose for healthcare power of attorney, or it might be someone else. As with naming a guardian and trustee, you should have one main designee for your powers of attorney, along with two to three backup names.

"Wait — " you might be thinking. "I need to pick people to be guardians, trustees, my healthcare power of attorney, and my durable power of attorney? And I need multiple options for each?"

Most people name the same person for multiple roles, to keep things from becoming too confusing. For instance, your son might be financially smart and trustworthy; you might choose him to act as your trustee *and* your durable power of attorney, because those roles both deal with finances. (If you choose two different people for those roles, a durable power of attorney does not override who you named as a trustee on your trust.) Maybe your daughter is a nurse, so you make her your healthcare power of attorney. We recommend naming two or three backups in case the original cannot or will not act.

Final Disposition

Less legally binding than the living will and powers of attorney are the final disposition and the ethical will. Both of these documents are primarily values-oriented, and relate to your desires and wishes.

The final disposition describes your funeral wishes. Do you want a somber affair, or a "celebration of life" party? Do you want an elaborate casket or a simple one? Do you want your ashes spread out over Lake Michigan? Would you like certain songs, speakers, or readings to be featured in your service? A final disposition isn't required, nor should it be your first priority. However, it can be a comfort to your family for them to know they're giving you the memorial that you'd want.

Ethical Will

If there's anything "warm and fuzzy" about documents related to your death, it would be the ethical will. Like the final disposition, your ethical will is not a contractual document. **The ethical will is where you discuss your wishes for your family, and your hopes for what comes next.**

For example, you might want to leave a video which talks about the history of your family business. Maybe you include letters written to each family member, telling them what you value most in them, and what you hope for their future. Perhaps you include the story of how your grandfather built his wealth, and specific ideas for how you'd like your children and grandchildren to carry on his legacy. You might codify your personal value system, or share observations about how the Family Vision has morphed over the generations.

The ethical will is values-oriented, with a focus on storytelling and family history. For an excellent resource to learn more about crafting a meaningful ethical will (along with many other helpful tips in estate planning), check out *Creating the Good Will,* by Elizabeth Arnold.

YOUR LAST GIFT

All of us want to "end well." We want to be remembered fondly, and most of us want to bless the people and organizations we love, even after we go.

For many, the grief and confusion which follow a loved one's passing can be consuming. Without the companionship and trust of a partner, people can struggle to make clear-minded decisions. Also, if the bereaved family member wasn't the dominant financial decision-maker, the financial components of settling an estate can feel overwhelming. For all these reasons, we want to encourage you to take steps to make this process *easier* for the people you love.

We've suggested that you **communicate** with your family as you get the ball rolling with formulating an estate plan. We also highly recommend that you **bring your children and spouse along to meetings with your financial advisor.** That way, when a crisis hits, family members at least *know who to call,* in regard to finances. There's a place to begin which is familiar and nonthreatening.

Nate and Shannon[34] are a perfect example of why coming to meetings together can be so valuable. Nate was diagnosed with Pancreatic cancer in his mid-50s. In their marriage, Nate was always the one to handle finances—but when he got his diagnosis, he and Shannon proactively worked to acquaint her with their full financial picture. We completed the Personal Wealth Organizer together with them. For the next eighteen months, Shannon came to every meeting. She had the benefit of learning about their finances while Nate was still present to indicate his opinions and approval. He was able to explain his vision behind the various accounts and his methods for managing the money.

When Nate died, Shannon, of course, felt enormous grief. But in the midst of the memorial preparations, paperwork, and emotional pain, there was one thing Shannon *didn't* have to worry about: everything regarding their finances

---

34 Names have been changed.

was already taken care of. She knew exactly what next steps to take. After Nate's funeral, we were able to hug her and encourage her to take all the time she needed to process his death. There was no urgency for her to sort out their finances; much of the work had already been taken care of.

Not every family has the luxury of being able to anticipate a passing, like Nate and Shannon. However, in our opinion, this fact makes it that much more crucial to establish the financial picture ahead of time. Before the crisis hits, family members need to know some key basics of the financial picture.

Stories like Terri Schiavo's, or even our client who brought in the bag full of random documents, remind us that it is a challenge to assemble all the details necessary to close up a life. Hear us when we say, *this is worth it*. The Personal Wealth Organizer ensures that you are maximizing your financial potential while you are still living—but its most significant impact may come after you pass. In the last fifteen years, we've seen some incredibly emotional reactions when we give a Personal Wealth Organizer to clients or to the surviving family members of one of our clients. People feel unbelievable relief to have such a substantial burden lifted.

For us, with our kids—and for you, with your loved ones— this is truly our last gift to them. They'll have to make the transition to living life without us, one way or another. We can help them travel that road by paving the way.

CHAPTER SEVEN

———

DANGEROUS BIASES, BEHAVIORS, AND CIRCUMSTANCES

"Before you talk, listen. Before you react, think. Before you spend, earn. Before you quit, try."

ERNEST HEMINGWAY

Cäcilie Albrecht, the "grand-dame" of the $40 billion Aldi supermarket fortune, died in November of 2018. She and her husband, Theo, had formed a Family Vision. They'd seen their son take up that vision and conduct himself as a family steward. She'd written a will which clearly designated her wishes for her estate.

And yet, the Albrecht family is now engulfed in a massive feud. Cäcilie specified in her will that her daughter-in-law, who has survived her late son, should be cut out of the estate and disallowed from any participation in business decisions.

She also cut out her five grandchildren. Her criticism? All of them, in her opinion, indulged in lavish spending.

Reportedly, she wrote in her will:

> "With this document I undertake to ensure the preservation of the philosophy of our family, which is to serve the consortium Aldi Nord and to foster this, at the same time as setting aside self-interests and practicing a modest and abstemious way of life."[35]

Cäcilie's daughter-in-law and grandchildren had apparently proven that they could not be trusted to live into the "modest and abstemious" lifestyle the Albrecht family wanted to be known for, and showed a pattern of irresponsibility in their business practices. Therefore, the matriarch cut them out.

What happened? This story begins like a textbook example of a family that was doing it *right*—and yet, the fortune and family responsibilities were not passed on to the third generation; they were passed *over*.

In spite of your best efforts and intentions, your ability to pass on your wealth and values to the people you love can still be thwarted if there are dangerous biases or behaviors at work. For instance, in the story of the Albrecht family, we can see that the Self-Control Bias—which we'll discuss

---

35 Connolly, Kate. "Late Grand Dame of Aldi Clan Sparks Family Feud with Her Will." The Guardian. Guardian News and Media, April 2, 2019. https://www.theguardian.com/business/2019/apr/02/late-grand-dame-of-aldi-clan-sparks-family-feud-with-her-will.

in depth in this chapter—was likely in place, which led to irresponsible financial habits among the (would-be) heirs.

For a successful experience in passing it on, it is crucial that you and your heirs understand these potential dangers, evaluate where they might be present in your family, and work to root them out through communication or cognitive therapy.

Most often, these dangerous biases and behaviors stem from an emotional root. Even when facts and logic should be the louder voice, emotions can be the leading factor in decision making. Often, these emotional biases can lead people to make financial decisions which ultimately would undermine an estate's growth or ability to pass wealth on.

In this chapter, we want to acquaint you with some of these dangerous biases and behaviors. *Recognizing* them may not make the hard emotions any easier to deal with. However, if there's no awareness of the dangers that might be lurking in the shadows, you have no ability to guard against them. We want to do everything possible to set you up for a successful "passing it on," so we're going to take this chapter to educate you about the common pitfalls we've seen that can sabotage the success of family stewardship.

You might be guilty of harboring one or several of these dangers. Perhaps, as you read, you'll recognize the dangers as existing in some of your family members. Once you identify where these dangers may lurk, you can do something about it. If you *know* your biases, you have the power to consider whether or not you want to continue down the path you're on. If you remain *unaware* of your behavioral and emotional biases, your decisions about money will be informed by those biases—and not necessarily what's objectively best for your estate or your family.

Reviewing these different biases won't make it any easier to discard emotions in a major financial decision. However, we believe that **if you make yourself aware of these behavioral and emotional biases, you will be better equipped to make objective decisions about your money.**

DANGEROUS BIASES

If you operate with a bias, you're not able to evaluate an investment in the same way you would a comparable opportunity. You give your favored investment the benefit of the doubt in every scenario. Your lens is skewed. The rational quantitative evaluation that you would normally use in your financial decisions is thrown out the window.

Here are some of the specific lens-bending biases people might operate with. Consider whether or not any of these might describe an unknown bias influencing you.

THE ENDOWMENT BIAS

Imagine you've inherited a piece of land. It's on a swamp, in a flood plain. The house on the property has mold in the basement and a roof covered in moss. This property is a liability. The smart financial move would be to off-load it as soon as possible, but you won't. Why?

Let's say this house is where your mom grew up. She's told you stories of exploring the grasses in the swamp, and catching frogs. Now that your mom is gone, you can't imagine parting with this property—even if it is going to drain your savings. You value the *connection* to your family more than you do the appreciation or depreciation of the asset.

This, essentially, is the Endowment Bias, also known as the Endowment Effect. **The Endowment Bias shows up every time you're unable to make objective financial decisions because of an emotional tie to an asset.** Behavioral Economics explains, "This bias occurs when we *overvalue* something that we own, regardless of its objective market value (Kahneman, et al., 1991)."[36]

Put simply, take the emotional layer out of the equation, and the wise financial decision becomes clear. But when an asset feels attached to something you value emotionally—a person, a piece of advice, a wonderful memory, and so on—it becomes much more challenging to recognize the best financial path forward.

Strategies to Overcome the Endowment Bias

We understand the significance of the emotions that come into play with the Endowment Bias. When adult children are trying to decide how to handle their deceased parents' estate, of *course* they would be focused on how best to honor their parents' legacy.

To make these emotionally loaded financial decisions a little

---

36 "Endowment Effect: Behavioral Economics.com: The BE Hub."
Behavioraleconomics.com | The BE Hub. March 28, 2019. Accessed August 13, 2019. https://www.behavioraleconomics.com/resources/mini-encyclopedia-of-be/endowment-effect/, our emphasis.

easier, we recommend you recognize that the *original* value of the asset you're dealing with came about during a different time. Market conditions were different; real estate conditions were different; family conditions were different. Your benefactor gained this asset by doing what he or she thought was best for the family, at that particular time.

Take that same spirit — doing what's best for your family — and use that as your motivator for determining what to do with this asset. Times *have* changed. It's possible that the best way to honor your parent or grandparent is to handle that investment in the same savvy way they might have, were they still alive to reckon with these new conditions.

We have one client who was able to get over the endowment bias, adjust her portfolio to what makes sense for the current times, and still beautifully honors her father's legacy through philanthropy. She worked hard to perpetuate the family estate, and as her money grew, she gave to charities that she knew her father supported or would have loved. In that way, she was able to honor the emotional tie of the assets he'd left her, while also having the freedom to allow the estate to change under new market conditions.

Secondly, your financial decision-making process might also be helped if you actually make it a *process*. **If you have a mechanical methodology for making financial decisions, that methodology can help erode some of the emotional ties that might otherwise confuse you.**

Here's one example of a process you could use which incorporates stress testing (a process we discussed in chapter five):

1. Ascertain your goal. ("I need $200,000 a year in income.")
2. Develop a financial and investment plan that will help you achieve your goal.
3. Stress test your plan against changing variables within your situation to find the breaking point and make sure you are comfortable with your current strategy.
4. Reevaluate every few years.

A process like this can help offset dangerous biases, because you're identifying goals that are more thoughtful of your future and creating practical steps to get there. They can make the decision-making process more mechanical, and help you direct your efforts toward a worthwhile vision for your future.

STATUS QUO BIAS

The Status Quo Bias can show up in every area of life and can be summed up in a few words: you do what you've always done. Rather than make healthy, needed changes, you keep operating with the current state of affairs. Sometimes, people fear that they'll make a mistake if they make any changes. You might think that if you don't do anything, you'll be okay; if you make any decision, it could be the wrong decision. That's an understandable fear—but unfortunately, *not* making a decision is, in itself, a decision! And quite possibly, one that could do you more harm than good in the long run.

Just about everyone can identify the Status Quo Bias in some area of life. Maybe you stick with the same workout routine because you don't want to bother figuring out a new one, even though your body is showing signs of strain.

You keep the same meals on rotation, because it feels like too much work to look up new recipes and buy unfamiliar ingredients.

Change can be hard and inconvenient. Often, it requires putting in time or further education and overcoming a fear of change. Maybe you don't want to venture outside of your comfort zone because you're afraid you might struggle and get negative feedback. However, change can also be good and necessary. When you're dealing with money, getting yourself out of the Status Quo Bias can open you up to new opportunities and result in positive changes.

The Status Quo Bias can impact many areas of financial decision making. Here are just a few examples of how they can play out—and why the Status Quo Bias rightly fits the description of "dangerous":

- You make an investment in stocks but never scrutinize their status. You might wake up one day and discover that your investment has gone to zero.
- You have a collection of five 401(k)s from five different jobs. It's difficult to keep track of them all, manage them all—and sometimes even hard to *remember* them all. Through not monitoring or consolidating those accounts, you easily run the risk of wasting investment opportunities or even losing some of that hard-earned money altogether.
- You inherit a portfolio of CDs and bonds. That investment strategy may have worked for your grandmother, so you leave it. However, as market conditions change, financial strategies need to change. An investment that is appropriate for your grandmother's time horizon

may not work for *your* time horizon. If you leave it unchanged, you run the risk of losing money, and/or could lose out on better investment opportunities.

• You inherit a business, and the business seems to be running well, so you decide to be hands-off. In a few years, bad management has run the business into the ground, and your investment in the business has now tanked.

• You purchase an apartment building, put it under the care of a property manager, and leave it at that. With no active involvement on your part, you have no idea if the property manager is doing a bad job, or if the neighborhood starts to decline in value. Once again, your investment could tank.

• You experience an enormous stroke of luck—maybe a stock you bought at $5 shoots up to $100, or a house you bought at the bottom of the market triples in value—and you can't bring yourself to cash in on the investment. You hope that the "lucky" investment will keep growing, even though that may be unrealistic. Your best window for selling ultimately passes you by.

• You wrote your estate plan a decade ago and haven't revisited it since. In the past ten years, you've had new grandchildren born, and one of your children has gotten divorced from their spouse. Under your current plan, some of the people you most love will get nothing, and some of the people who are no longer in your life are set to inherit large sums of your money.

The emotion at the root of the financial Status Quo Bias is often a simple one: you might just be **distracted** from the busy pace of your life. Taking the time to research market conditions seems unrealistic, given your current packed schedule of work, family, and other obligations. Or, perhaps you're **intimidated** by the knowledge that would be required to adequately step up your management of your retirement account investments. You might feel **afraid** of making a mistake, so you do nothing.

Sometimes, the emotion behind the Status Quo Bias might be more complicated. When we work with clients on estate planning and wills, people have to start thinking about their own deaths. That's uncomfortable—it brings up fear, sadness, grief, and hard evaluations of the people you love. In this case, the Status Quo Bias might be motivated by **reluctance to deal with a painful topic**.

In all these scenarios, we fall into the Status Quo Bias because it feels *easier*. Operating on autopilot can be a danger to your finances, estate, and family. Having a well-defined process and hiring the right team can resolve the Status Quo Bias because your team can bring the expertise and experience to help you make informed decisions. Here are a few other strategies that can help.

Strategies to Overcome the Status Quo Bias

To overcome the Status Quo Bias, first consider what may be at the root. Is your issue one of fear? Busyness? Reluctance to deal with a sad topic? Once you determine the root of your personal Status Quo Bias, you might be able to determine strategies to deal with it, like some of the following.

For people who feel too busy or lack knowledge to change their investment status quo, consider this easy option: many retirement or college investment plans have an age-based option, sometimes referred to as a **"target date-based fund."** Essentially, you indicate how far into the future you'll need your money, and then the investment company makes those allocation decisions for you, based on your projected timeframe. In these cases, it's okay if you don't understand the industry: the people that do will manage your money for you.

You'll get an even more personalized approach if you **enlist the help of an expert, like a financial advisor or attorney.** As financial advisors, it's our job to help our clients through some of these hard processes. Sometimes our clients give us a hard time when we call them up and remind them of a document we're waiting on or check in to see if they finalized their estate plan—"No Mom, I haven't done it yet," they joke. However, they know it is incredibly helpful to have someone specifically assigned to pull them along about taking such needed steps. A trusted advisor will understand your busy schedule and life's demands, but they're still going to pull you along to help you achieve the goals you have set for yourself.

Supportive, knowledgeable professionals can be instrumental in helping you overcome whatever emotions might be at the root of your Status Quo Bias. Reference the "Assembling Your Team" section in the Appendix for recommendations on finding these people.

SELF-CONTROL BIAS

Live for today and don't think about tomorrow! That, in a nutshell, is the Self-Control Bias. If you see a gorgeous new car on the lot, you buy it, and don't consider how that might impact your long-term goals. When it comes to money, you act in the moment. Your decisions are directed more by impulses, than by discipline or self-control.

Cäcilie Albrecht's criticism of her daughter-in-law, Babette, was focused on her lavish spending. Babette, supposedly, funneled money out of the Aldi business to support her luxurious lifestyle, which would make her an obvious candidate for the Self-Control Bias. However, the bias can show up in more subtle ways than just big spending.

Imagine a parent who gives their children whatever they ask for. They might know their children will become spoiled, but the parent just can't help indulging their kids, so the money spigot never turns off. Here, too, the tendency is to give in to impulsive emotions, rather than keep long-term goals in mind.

The Self-Control Bias can be an Achilles' heel for children who have grown up wealthy. They might be used to living a luxurious lifestyle and expect to continue living large until they die. Take Sarah, for instance, another hypothetical character who makes some of the common mistakes in this category. Sarah grew up in a wealthy family, and had her parents wrapped around her finger. They regularly purchased her the things she asked for. Now, as an adult, Sarah has a great salary and gets additional income from her trust fund. Still—she spends beyond that. She wants to live in a luxury home, drive luxury cars, and use luxury products. When she gets a large monetary gift from her parents, she spends it almost immediately. She hasn't ever had to practice managing or saving money, so there's no discipline developed in how she manages that gift. She knows she needs to save if she wants to eventually retire, but those considerations don't change her spending habits in the meantime.

People like Sarah can put themselves in a dangerous position if they lose their job, or the well goes dry. As financial advisors, we're able to calculate the drain of a person's spending habits on their estate and estimate when the money will run out. However, if someone like Sarah grows up with the spigot always turned on, it can be hard to imagine it will ever turn off. Especially if there's a large inheritance at play, people feel like the money will continue forever and they want to enjoy their lifestyles.

We fully endorse living a life you'll enjoy—but we also endorse having enough to sustain your family's needs for a lifetime and passing on wealth to future generations. Those three goals can coexist, provided you swap out the Self-Control Bias for disciplined goal-setting.

Several emotions can be at the root of the Self-Control Bias. **Insecurity** might be at play. If money feels tied to your self-worth, you're going to spend money whenever you want a boost. There might be a real fear that, if you stop spending money the way you do, people won't want to be around you anymore.

Some people truly believe they'll **die young** and want to live well while they're still here. **Entitlement** can be an issue: "My family runs this town. Our name is on the buildings. I should get to benefit from their contributions." Sometimes, as we've described, people **don't know the limits of their estate,** and operate like the money is limitless.

The Self-Control Bias can also operate when you have a **limited view of your contribution.** If you have a stable job, you might feel like that's "enough" of a societal contribution. You might assume you don't have to work at financial independence. You're not thinking about *growing* your wealth, or contributing in a bigger way to your community; instead, you might just focus on retiring early and living it up.

Strategies to Overcome the Self-Control Bias

If you would prefer to make a change in how you handle finances, but have struggled to bring your spouse or children along, consider having the Family Vision conversation, covered in chapter one. If you've already had it and there's still an obvious lack of self-control in your family members' spending, have the conversation again. Getting on the same page about the purpose of money will be an important first step toward healthy change. Consider ways you can implement steps of accountability for changing behavior to better align with the vision.

Many of the values and disciplines we've discussed throughout this book work as an antidote to the self-control bias. Review some of the strategies we've suggested to help engender the values of family stewardship: habits of delayed gratification, long-term goal setting, gratitude, and generosity.

DANGEROUS BEHAVIORS

Dangerous *biases* have to do with the ways our emotions can confuse our financial decision-making. But then what happens? Dangerous decision-making can lead to financially dangerous *behaviors*. Here are some of the dangerous behaviors we've seen that can easily drain your bank accounts.

MISPLACED TRUST

Bernie Madoff. Enron. Charles Ponzi. What do they all have in common? They all lost millions of dollars for people who trusted in them.

Putting your trust in the wrong person, strategy, or institution is one of the most dangerous financial behaviors you can fall into. Negative influencers don't just show up on the front pages though, like Bernie Madoff. People take financial advice from other people all the time, be it a news story, an uncle's tip about a hot stock, or a colleague's "winning strategy" which he tells you about at the water cooler.

Most people have all kinds of financial questions they're seeking answers for: "When should I start taking my pension?" "Should I take a survivor benefit or not?" "Should I take the pension as a lump sum or income stream?" "When should I start taking Social Security?" If a friend or a favorite news anchor offers an apparent answer to your question—it's accepted as factual truth.

Bits of advice that float our way feel authentic and trustworthy. However, it's rare that a financial tip will take into consideration your age, station in life, financial goals, financial needs, and current financial position. Sometimes even good advice may not be good advice for *you*.

Jim Cramer is a famed TV personality and stock picker and *may* give a solid stock tip on his TV show. However, you need a working knowledge about how to take a stock recommendation and fit it into your whole picture before following his advice. The guy that happens to sit down to eat dinner in front of Cramer's show might think, "I better go do this! It's going to get me to retirement." However, that's not necessarily true.

What if that gentleman has a daughter who gets seizures and he has to fund enormous medical bills? What if his other child is in college? What if he also needs to fund his own retirement? Jim Cramer doesn't know the specific details about the people's lives who hear his advice. You might feel inspired by another person's overconfidence, and follow advice that's a bad choice for your particular situation.

Consider *your* particular situation. If someone tells you that you've got to start taking your Social Security at age sixty-two, try stress testing that scenario. Consider what your finances would look like if you waited until you were sixty-five to start taking Social Security. Would that improve your financial picture? It might. However, if you're terminally ill, it probably wouldn't—in that case, you should collect your Social Security as soon as possible. The right move depends on your unique position in life.

When bits of advice come your way, let them inspire you to explore new possibilities. Grab ahold of those nuggets, and listen—but know that the advice may not always work well for your particular situation. That information should be vetted before you consider it a sure thing.

Be wary of potential bad actors out there who present

themselves as an unbiased financial resource, but are actually intent on selling you a product. Get a second or third opinion before confidently following one person's recommendation.

Strategies to Overcome the Misplaced Trust Behavior

Before taking advice from a potentially negative influence, lay out the full picture of your finances. Consider your resources, your health situation, your family situation, your long-term goals, and values. When the entire picture is assembled, *then* you can start quantitative analysis and stress testing, and make decisions from there.

One of the best ways you can help guard yourself against negative influences and get the help you need, is to assemble a group of advisors in your life. Ideally, these would be professionals who have a broad range of perspectives and experience. Reference our guide for finding trustworthy experts in our Appendix.

ENTITLEMENT RUT: LORI NARRATES

When I was in college, I didn't have an ATM card. Every week, I'd have to think methodically about how much I would need for spending, go to the bank, and withdraw the cash I would need.

But I had a friend who had a different approach. I liked this friend—he was funny and easy going. He *did* have an ATM card. I remember hanging out with him once when he withdrew some money and he cheerfully commented, "My parents are going to have to fill that back up! It's running low." I remember seeing that his balance at the time was $1,500, which seemed like a huge amount to me.

I think his parents thought they were supporting my friend; they expected that he would be able to spend more time focusing on his studies if he wasn't obligated to work. The reality was, with no skin in the game, my friend didn't seem motivated to do well in his classes. If he failed a class, it was no problem to ask his parents to pay for another round. They were wealthy enough that there was no pressure for him to make money any time soon, and he didn't seem interested in choosing a major. At times I wondered if his lack of direction had anything to do with never *needing* a direction. There was always plenty in the bucket to draw from, and no hurry to get anywhere.

Although we work with many wealthy families who financially support their kids and still teach their kids to be incredibly hard working, we also can see the easy trap of the **Entitlement Rut,** another dangerous behavior. When a generation **loses touch with the sacrifice** that another generation made, the younger generation can develop an attitude of entitlement. This can easily sap their motivation, limit their contribution, and discourage their desire to learn financial smarts.

Merriam-Webster defines entitlement as "the belief that one is inherently deserving of privileges or special treatment." If you come to believe you're **inherently deserving** of special treatment, you can easily slip into negative mentalities, like the Self-Control Bias. You also tend to **focus on yourself,** more than on others, which can lead to a lack of fulfillment.

Sometimes, the Entitlement Rut can come about from

misperceptions about how much wealth heirs should expect to receive. We sometimes hear elderly parents tell their adult children, "I'm leaving you plenty. You'll be fine. You won't have to worry about money." Parents intend to be comforting when they say this, but often, their children get inflated ideas in their heads about how much they can expect. When an estate is split among multiple children and grandchildren, possibly taxed, and potentially reduced from legal fees, adult children can end up with a much smaller piece of the pie than they expected.

In some cases, the adult children have set themselves up to *rely* on a larger financial gift than they receive. They might have a hefty mortgage, or didn't bother putting aside money for their kids' college education. Maybe they chose a career that didn't pay well, because they expected to make up the difference with their inheritance. They may not have bothered to educate themselves in financial literacy, assuming they wouldn't need to worry about making money. That can be dangerous—for both the adult children, and their own children.

Here are some other ways the Entitlement Rut can set heirs up for failure:

- Larger-than-life spending will result in a **rapidly eroding estate**. Even if heirs can sustain themselves on their inheritance, they won't end up leaving much (if anything) to their children.
- People living in the Entitlement Rut often end up feeling **a lack of fulfillment**. They're not using their skills toward any meaningful contribution, and that can end up leading to frustration or disappointment.

- Someone acting with the Entitlement Rut may also end up in **real financial jeopardy** toward the end of life. If they run out of money, and haven't worked for most of their adult life, they'll struggle to get a job. They'll also likely struggle to live with financial restraint.

Strategies to Overcome the Entitlement Rut

First, **share and surround**. One of our clients has done an amazing job preventing the Entitlement Rut in his own kids. These children have inherited enormous sums of money, but they've remained grounded and responsible. Their dad practices our recommendation of *sharing stories:* he constantly reminds them where the money came from. Leading up to the point where the children started controlling the assets, their dad regularly invited his children to attend meetings with us and included them on many discussions. He continues to *surround* them with grounding influences, and it's paying off. The children have never made a single withdrawal from their financial assets. In their minds, those assets are for their future, and more importantly, for future generations.

When money is gifted with few or no expectations—like my friend in college—that's when the entitlement rut can set in. But **good communication** can help your children use that money in responsible, successful ways—building it and prolonging it, just like we've seen with our client.

Finally, remember that **gratitude and generosity** can be part of the antidote to Entitlement. If you are seeing attitudes of entitlement in your children, start doing what you can to implement family traditions of giving.

ENABLING BEHAVIOR

Most people know the saying, "Don't give a man a fish; teach him how to fish." But as parents, this is sometimes easier said than done. We don't want to see our kids hurt or in pain; we want to protect them from making bad decisions. We want them to flourish, and ideally, we want them to get there without ever getting injured or struggling. Ironically though, by protecting our kids to that extent, we actually prevent them from experiencing the challenges they need to build up their own grit. We're *enabling* their dysfunction and immaturity.

Enabling Behavior is similar to the Entitlement Rut, but the Entitlement Rut refers to the *kids'* problem. Enabling Behavior refers to the *parents'* problem. Here are a few examples of how Enabling Behavior can play out, financially or otherwise:

- A child runs up thousands of dollars in credit card debt, and the parent agrees to pay it off. The child is not required to pay the parent back on any particular time frame or with interest—or at all.
- A child convinces their parent to go in on an investment with them—maybe a development property or a business. The investment tanks, and the parent never gets paid back.
- A parent writes their child's résumés, does their science fair projects, and negotiates with teachers to secure higher grades for their child every semester.
- Parents consistently buy their children's big ticket items: a house, a car, etc.

The motivation behind Enabling Behavior is a good one:

parents want to care for their children. Sometimes **guilt** is involved: If a parent knows that he or she easily *could* buy their child's dream house, why wouldn't they? That guilt can get in the way of good judgment if a kid keeps coming to the well and asking for money. The parent might think, "How can I sit here and deprive my child, when I have millions?" If divorce or family strain is part of the picture, the guilt can be even stronger—and the child may learn to use their parent's guilt to get what they want.

Wealthy people often **feel the need to provide** for those that they love, whether that's family or friends. This feels loving—but it can lead to unintended consequences.

If people come to expect consistent handouts, they're never held accountable for their actions. They don't have the opportunity to learn from their mistakes, or to gain needed lessons in financial literacy. Enabling Behavior can actually set up the people you love for making *more* mistakes—bigger mistakes—down the road.

Enabling Behavior can also lead to resentment. Parents can feel used if a child repeatedly asks them for money. They might also feel taken advantage of if a child never offers to repay a loan or a tanked investment.

Strategies to Overcome the Enabling Behavior

If your child comes to you and needs help, of course it is okay to help them. But we'd encourage you to be thoughtful about how you do so. Parents and grandparents should think about the following first:

1. Will giving to my children compromise my own quality of life or security?
2. Will there be tax consequences or penalties?
3. Will the gift have unintended consequences (i.e., funding a spendthrift habit or gambling)?

Going through those questions will help you open your eyes to the possible risks of your assistance and enable you to manage those risks accordingly.

Also, consider laying down some **rules.** We've seen successful families avoid Enabling Behavior through clear communication and boundaries. They may fund a loan for their children, but they have the kids pay them back at a low interest rate and on a specified time frame. We have also seen parents help fund Roth IRA contributions annually and have specific conversations to let the child know it is for retirement. Another path of support is to gift stock to your children over time, while also making a point to educate on investing, encourage them to build their retirement savings, and discuss the benefits of letting the stocks grow, rather than selling or spending in a hurry.

You could also consider using an **intermediary.** If your child comes to you with an investment opportunity, direct them to other investors or a bank. Those other people will more intently scrutinize the business plan, which will force your child to think through needed steps. Encourage your child to outline a specific plan of how they intend to turn a profit with dates, deadlines, and milestone projections. A third party can increase both the accountability factor, and the risk for your child—which could help them strengthen their efforts.

When your children are forced to take on the responsibility and consequences for their choices, you're pushing them to be more thoughtful, careful, and smart about how they use their money. That's loving!

OTHER DANGEROUS BEHAVIORS

Briefly, here are a few more dangerous behaviors that we sometimes witness[37]:

- **Overconfidence:** Overconfidence occurs when someone exaggerates the likelihood of a given strategy's success. Remember how Roger as a college student thought he had superior knowledge about technology stocks, so he invested most his capital there? That was a dangerous decision motivated by overconfidence—one that he hasn't made again! Overconfidence can result in dangerously concentrated positions and much higher risks—in your investment portfolio, or in other areas of financial investment. It also weakens your planning process, because your preconceived notions are amplified by your overconfidence. That can lead to bad decision-making.

- **Herd Behavior:** Herd behavior is what it sounds like: you go with the crowd, even if the crowd is making irrational decisions. Trends like Beanie Babies® or Tulip Mania attest to the power of herd behavior; the tech bubble in the early 2000s is a more sobering example. People don't want to miss out on a good thing, so they

---

37 Waserman, Kastle. "The Psychology of Client Behavior." New Age of Advice. March 27, 2019. Accessed July 08, 2019. https://www.transamerica.com/ financial-professional/what-we-offer/education/new-age-of-advice/article/ psychology-of-client-behavior.

follow the herd. People think, "Everybody else is doing it, so it must be a good idea." They buy stocks when everyone buys; they sell stocks when everyone sells. You can correct this behavior by *gathering evidence* about the move you want to make, and objectively consider whether or not it supports what you want to do. Having a good team of advisors in place and a mechanical decision-making process can also help prevent impulsive decisions based on what the herd is doing.

- **Anchoring**: Anchoring occurs when you pick a data point and make all your judgments based on that. Transamerica describes one example of how this could play out: "Your client may be ready to make a big ticket purchase, such as an engagement ring, and feel they need to go with a high price, such as the two-month salary 'rule' in order to 'do the right thing.'"[38] Or, let's say you pay $10 for a stock, and then it goes down to $5. Even if the market is clearly telling you otherwise, you had determined, based on your initial thesis, that $10 was the fair value for the company and won't sell until it's back to $10 or higher. If you stay anchored to one piece of data, you might make an unwise financial decision. Here's how to correct anchoring behavior: rather than anchoring to a piece of data that might not be relevant anymore, make your decision based on multiple data points and incorporating up-to-date information.

You might realize that your particular biases go deep and require specialized help. If that's the case, you're not alone. There's an entire industry of cognitive therapists devoted

---

38 Ibid

to helping people deal with their bad financial habits.[39] The fact that people get paid large sums of money to have therapeutic discussions about money reinforces that all these issues are real.

Although we've never worked with these therapists firsthand, we know from working with our clients that psychology is a major player in financial decisions. If you recognize that you have dangerous financial biases or behaviors, seeking out a financial therapist may not be a bad idea.

DANGEROUS CIRCUMSTANCES

Even the most emotionally grounded, disciplined person can still be thrown for a loop when a crisis hits. Like dangerous biases and behaviors, dangerous circumstances can also radically impact the financial picture. In chapter six, we discussed ways to help mitigate the challenges that can come from death, one of the hardest experiences life can throw at us.

In our work as financial advisors, we've seen two other events create huge financial challenges for families doing their best to pass it on: divorce and sudden wealth. Other smaller traumas, like the failure of a business or a prolonged illness, can also have a significant impact on your finances. Let's consider each of these, along with strategies to mitigate the fall out.

---

39 "How Cognitive Behavioral Therapy Can Prevent Poor Financial Choices." Money Crashers. December 26, 2018. Accessed July 08, 2019. https://www.moneycrashers.com/cognitive-behavioral-therapy-prevent-poor-financial-choices/.

DIVORCE

Divorce is emotionally hard and financially complicated. No matter who initiates the divorce or how messy it is, divorce can make your family's wealth vulnerable—especially if you have typically avoided dealing with your family's finances, and let your ex-spouse make most of the monetary decisions.

We worked with one woman—we'll call her Suzanne—who came to us in the midst of divorce proceedings. She and her husband had operated a successful business together, but the stress had taken a toll on their relationship. Although Suzanne had been well acquainted with the day-to-day operations of the business, she'd let her husband, a CPA, handle all of the finances. Suzanne didn't know the names of their accounts, their investments, or the details of their taxes.

Suzanne was already in a tough place, emotionally. She was facing the pain of losing her marriage and fighting for custody of her kids. She was trying to get acquainted with her family's financial picture and learn basic financial literacy about how each account worked. Now, she was facing his attorney who wanted to pressure her to give up many of the investments, and she didn't even know which ones to fight for. At one point, she told us she felt like she was curled up in the corner of the attorney's office, getting pummeled with artillery. This was not an ideal time for her to start learning about the details of her finances.

We got Suzanne through it. There was a lot of hand-holding, and we worked constantly with her over the next couple years to educate, educate, educate. She was able to pick up the pieces, move forward, and we can happily report that Suzanne is in a great spot now.

As a general rule, we insist that **couples come see us together at least once or twice a year,** to avoid scenarios where one spouse in a marriage is completely in the dark. Money is not an area where either spouse should be "siloed" out of the picture. The healthiest financial scenario for a marriage is to have two informed spouses.

However, in the worst-case scenario, a divorcing spouse may be in the dark when it comes to the family's finances. They may not even know that certain accounts exist. In the unfortunate case of divorce, **a divorce attorney will assist in retrieving financial information from your soon to be ex-spouse.**

Divorce can be even more complicated when you're dealing with **commingled families,** a.k.a. mixed families. Let's say Carla had two children from her first marriage and Richard had one; then they have two children together; then, they divorce, and Richard goes on to have one more child with his third wife. Which child gets how much? That inheritance picture is going to get complicated, fast.

If you find yourself in this position, the best thing you can do for your family is to have a documented plan for the inheritance. Maintain an updated estate plan and be as detailed as possible. Although this could require some tough decisions on your part, you'll be doing your family a tremendous favor by initiating them yourself, rather than leaving your loved ones to have those hard conversations in your absence—leaving room for interpretation can create animosity and foster greed.

If Your Children Get Divorced

Let's say that you're not worried about your own marriage, but you *are* concerned about your child's marriage. Considering how high divorce rates are, you may worry divorce could impact your child and want to establish some preemptive defenses.

There are estate planning measures for **creditor protection or divorce protection**.[40] For example, as a general rule, when you place an inheritance in a trust with limited access for your beneficiary's lifetime, you allow your beneficiary to receive distributions from the trust at the trustee's discretion, but the balance of the assets remains protected. In some cases the trust can protect the assets from dissipation in divorce because the trust helps clarify that the assets were inherited and never commingled in marital assets. Further, because the trustee is responsible for all distributions and the trustee is subject to a fiduciary duty (meaning, they have to act in the best financial interests of the beneficiary), the assets are not treated as owned by the beneficiary. Why would that be a good thing if your child gets divorced? If the assets are not owned by the beneficiary, they are generally not subject to equitable distribution.

This type of trust may also protect trust funds from creditors. For example, imagine your child gets in a car accident and there's not enough insurance to cover the damages; in that case, litigators might go after your child's personal assets. If the assets are kept in a trust with limited access,

---

40 Note: the rules applicable to creditor protection over trusts varies from state to state. If this tool sounds like something you'd like to pursue, consult with an attorney to learn more about your particular state's rules.

they may not only be less desirable to the creditor, but in some cases fully out of reach.

The best time to consider your child's future marital success might actually be before their marriage ever starts. Whether you love or hate your child's fiancé(e), it's not a bad idea to use the tool of a **premarital agreement** (commonly referred to as a prenuptial agreement, or "prenup"). A premarital agreement can insulate your child from inevitable financial risks, in the case of divorce, by listing out what each person owns and providing direction for what happens with the assets.

The terms "Separate Property" and "Community Property" might be useful to understand when drafting a premarital agreement. What is "Separate Property"? This definition depends on state law. Although each state is different, Separate Property usually includes assets inherited by the spouse, or in some cases assets that were obtained prior to the marriage (although timing doesn't always matter). In many states, a couple is able to define for themselves what is considered separate (thus, not subject to division in the event of a divorce), and what is marital; in some states the marital assets are called "Community Property," which generally would be divisible in a divorce.

Having a premarital agreement or assets held in a separate trust can help you avoid or at least mitigate this situation. With the help of an attorney, you can utilize these tools; that way, if your child does get divorced, there's a line in the sand regarding inherited assets.

If you feel concerns over the likelihood of your child's

future divorce, consider what steps you might want to take ahead of time to protect your child's financial future. Talk with your financial advisor and attorney about what provisions might be made to direct the money exactly where you want it to go. Do what you can to empower your child financially, introducing them to your financial advisor and equipping them with financial literacy. If they ultimately go through a divorce, they'll have some tools at their disposal to handle the financial ramifications.

Strategies to Ease the Financial Stress of Divorce

While you can't completely prevent all of these risks, you can take measures to mitigate potential risks. Here's a summarized list of our recommendations for how financial assets can be protected in the event of a divorce:

1. Spouses should both be **acquainted with the family's finances ahead of time,** if possible. If one spouse is in the dark about finances, that person should enlist a divorce attorney to track down the assets.
2. Pursue **financial literacy** for yourself and for your children.
3. Meet with **an experienced financial advisor** in the aftermath of divorce, to pursue additional financial education as needed and to make a game plan.
4. If you're concerned about your children getting divorced, and/or have a commingled family, work with your estate attorney to use **legal tools** to ensure the people you love receive the amount you want them to.
5. **Premarital agreements** or **separate trusts** can be used as tools to help protect wealth, should one of your children's marriages end in divorce.

THE CASE OF SUDDEN WEALTH

One of the most common "crises" we see clients encounter doesn't usually fit their idea of a crisis — usually, it starts off feeling like amazing good fortune. Handled poorly however, this "gift" can easily become a curse. We're talking about experiencing sudden wealth, which can come in many forms.

Business Insider published an article titled "20 Lottery Winners Who Lost Every Penny" which describes vividly the pain that can result from sudden wealth.[41] The article relays story after story of people who thought their wildest dreams had come true with their lottery win — only to later end up miserable and broke.

One couple bought their dream house and splurged on luxurious trips around Europe. Then, their underinsured house was ruined in a fire, and their marriage ultimately ended in divorce after suspected infidelity. Another man lost a third of his lottery winnings from being sued, and sunk the rest of his money into failing family businesses. His own brother put out a hit on him, hoping that he might inherit some of his brother's lottery winnings — yikes! Story after story describes mismanagement, family conflict, and pain.

Many people end up back where they were before the winning ticket, or in an even worse spot — for instance, in the second example just described, the man ended up over a million dollars in debt. Many people experience sudden wealth like a five-year-old kid would experience being left alone in a candy store. That child is going to go ballistic,

---

41 Abadi, Mark. "20 Lottery Winners Who Lost Every Penny." Business Insider. March 21, 2019. Accessed July 17, 2019. https://www.businessinsider.com/lottery-winners-lost-everything-2017-8.

gulp down treats as fast as he can, and then end up feeling sick!

Sudden wealth can come from winning millions in the lottery, but we more often see sudden wealth come via an inheritance from family. In both cases, the abrupt influx of wealth can be disorienting for the people who receive it—even hazardous to their financial stability and family's well-being. It is disappointing and devastating to see such an opportunity go to waste, and watch the next generation start from the ground up all over again.

Many of the worst dangers of inheriting sudden wealth can be avoided with good advice and financial education. We worked with a young man named Sam[42], who was in his early twenties when his parents tragically died. After their deaths, Sam was left with several million across Roth IRAs, traditional IRAs, and trust accounts. However, he had no team in place to help him handle that money.

In the US, when a person inherits IRAs, the government requires them to remove a certain amount from the account each year. If they fail to take the required minimum distribution, they are penalized 50 percent. Like most young twenty-somethings, Sam didn't know this. For three years, he didn't meet the requirements.

Since being introduced, we've worked hard to help Sam move forward, hiring a CPA to untangle his situation. Both of us have been impressed with his common sense; many young people would have blown through that money.

---

42 Name and some details have been changed for the sake of privacy.

Sam essentially didn't touch it, wary of making mistakes. However, as he realized, leaving his inheritance alone still produced problems.

Sam is smart, but initially, he didn't know which questions to ask. Obviously, he never expected to lose his parents when he was so young. Neither he nor his parents had prepared for him to handle a large inheritance on his own. Because of his lack of financial training, he struggled to find a team of professionals to help him when the tragic time did come.

Right now, Sam is at law school, studying to be a patent attorney. He's done well in his classes, and he's done well handling his finances. Sam sees his inheritance as a means to invest in his human capital in a way he couldn't have done otherwise. In his mind, his inheritance gives him a foundation for impacting the world. We love that.

Sam has landed on his feet, thanks to a lot of common sense and finding a highly experienced team of advisors. However, many children of wealthy parents could easily get into trouble when receiving a sudden large inheritance.

Here are some of the specific dangers that can come from sudden wealth:

- **Wrong assumptions about how long the wealth will last.** Imagine someone has always been a moderate wage earner. When they suddenly inherit a million dollars, they might think that'll be enough to last them for the rest of their lives. When it comes to sudden wealth, there's a common misperception about how long a sum of money will last. We see many cases where the value of that money is mismanaged, or not maximized, because the wealth feels like it will last forever.

- **You might become a target.** When a person or couple experiences sudden wealth, they might start to brag about it. As a general rule, bragging is a bad idea. We know of many stories about people who were taken advantage of by friends, family members, and acquaintances. Remember the Enabling Bias? People can easily feel guilted into giving money away and fail to steward it wisely.

- **You might be taken advantage of.** People who are newly wealthy can be viewed as easy prey for financial sharks—i.e., dishonest people who want to convince you to let them handle your money. Sudden wealth can also inspire people to come up with reasons to sue you.

- **Marital friction.** If you and your spouse have different visions for your wealth, having millions of dollars suddenly pour into your bank account can create enormous conflict. Imagine one person wants to spend money on a new house or car, while their spouse wants to save. This is breeding ground for marital friction—but it doesn't have to be. Having the discussion about Family Vision which we discussed in chapter one can help you get on the same page.

- **Mishandling the assets.** If a person who has suddenly inherited large wealth doesn't have strong financial literacy or is listening to the wrong people, they can easily mismanage their new wealth. There's poor planning, and poor investing. They might miss out on opportunities, or make losing investments. They might trust the wrong people, give too much away, or allow themselves to be taxed beyond belief.

Strategies to Cope with Sudden Wealth

Most of the dangers just described can be summarized singularly: unless people are educated well in advance on how to manage money, how to maximize opportunity, how to mitigate risks, and how to find an appropriate team of advisors, they can easily be played by sharks or make uninformed decisions.

Therefore, your best bet to equipping either yourself or your children to handle sudden wealth is to **focus on building up financial smarts and get a good team of advisors in place.** Reference our Appendix for recommendations on how to build a trustworthy team of advisors.

SOFTER TRAUMAS AND SHARKS

The financial picture can still alter radically from "softer traumas," like the failure of a business, corporate downsizing, medical diagnosis and treatment, or a major injury. Your main source of income may suddenly dry up, which can create enormous stress—both financially, and personally.

People who have practiced living independently and within their means are typically in a much better position to handle financial stress. Having a trusted financial team to support you can also be a game-changer when you are confronted with "softer trauma" situations. You'll also be better equipped to guard yourself against sharks—people who may recognize your financial naïveté and try to take advantage of that for their financial gain.

When we have taught classes, we'd have people ask us to analyze their personal financial situations. Sadly, many of these people would have the majority of their assets locked up in contractual products with surrender penalties, meaning they probably trusted a professional who was selling them a biased product. Consequently, they were faced with various costs and their money was tied up for great lengths of time.

It's possible that these professionals may have been genuinely knowledgeable. However, when we evaluated these people's finances, it became clear that these products didn't have their whole wealth management picture in mind and were actually causing real financial strain to some of the people we spoke to.

We knew a woman who would have been an easy target for a "shark." She was wealthy, but uninformed about her finances, which her husband had largely handled. After he passed away, the woman set up an estate plan which ultimately donated a third of her inheritance to a college. Here's the strange part: the woman had no association with that college. She didn't go there; her husband hadn't gone there; none of her children had gone there. However, her attorney who drafted her estate plan sat on the board of that college.

Unfortunately, we don't have enough details to know whether she truly valued what that school was doing for the community or whether the attorney coerced her into donating that money. We'd like to give her attorney the benefit of the doubt—but the story also makes clear the point that some people could be persuaded to make major financial decisions which may or may not reflect their true wishes.

Pay especially close attention to any financial product that would lock up your money for decades. Some of these products are marketed by "sharks" and pay a large commission fee. Although they may seem to come with appealing bells and whistles, these products may not always serve your whole financial picture or goals. If you're thinking of investing in a product like this, we encourage you to get financial advice from someone you trust, such as your financial advisor.

You can also help safeguard yourself against "sharks" by seeking out an unbiased financial advisor with transparent costs. Some people market themselves as financial advisors but actually make money by selling products to you, which may not actually serve your goals. A financial advisor with professional designations, who doesn't earn the bulk of their money from product commission, is a safer source for financial advice. Don't be afraid to ask pointed questions about costs; if your advisor is legitimate, they'll willingly be upfront with you about what you're paying for. We discuss more about what to look for in a financial advisor in our Appendix.

HELMETS AND HOCKEY PADS

The two of us love watching our kids play hockey. They look adorable getting dressed up in their thick pads and helmets and skates. Off the ice, their movement is clumsy, but when they're on the ice—all that padding is exactly what they need. They're able to confidently go on offense against their opponents, and they're protected against the hits that come their way.

In fact, without that thick padding, our kids wouldn't

manage to get very far as hockey players. Even if they know all the plays, even if they have great technique—without that protective gear, they're not going to be able to play.

In this book, we've tried to give you all kinds of coaching about good techniques and great plays. We've tried to give you recommendations on strategies and provided activities to hone your family's financial skills. We've gone over ways to build up your financial literacy, engender the values of family stewardship, and take practical steps to pass on your wealth.

But imagine how senseless it would be for a hockey coach to drill in strategy, technique, and skill to their players—and then push them out onto the ice with no helmets or padding. If they're not protected, then all the effort those players have put into learning the game could be cancelled out in a second with one solid hit from an opponent.

In this chapter, we've tried to essentially hand you some padding—some thick armor that will help protect you against the dangers you could pose to yourself, and the dangers that could come from outside of you. If you *recognize* that the dangers are real, then you'll take steps to protect yourself against them.

Take a good look at those potential dangers and put on some armor. As you prepare to play the game, make sure you're protected against the hits that could come. Financial smarts and healthy values will help you deal with many of the biases and behaviors that can otherwise jeopardize your financial decisions. Also, a trusted team of advisors, along with strategic use of legal tools, can help protect your estate from dangerous circumstances.

When our kids have their protective gear on, they have more confidence to play hard. They can take risks, because they've insulated themselves against getting hurt. By protecting your family against these various dangers, you'll help everyone have more fun and play a better game.

CONCLUSION

"Knowledge is only potential power. It becomes power only when, and if, it is organized into definite plans of action, and directed to a definite end."

NAPOLEON HILL

They had been quiet. Suspiciously quiet, for a suspiciously long amount of time.

Just as we started wondering what on earth Anna and Will were doing, the two of them came marching down the stairs with a Mason jar, stuffed to the brim with cash.

"We're going to save for a dirt bike together," Anna announced. "We're almost there. Look at all this money!" The jar was filled with coins. Our optimistic future dirt-bikers weren't even close!

But then Anna said something which made our jaws drop. She turned to Will—who, no doubt, had been the main force in convincing Anna that she suddenly wanted a dirt bike—and laid down the law. "We're doing this together this year," she informed him, "but next year, I need to start saving up my own money for college."

In the span of a few seconds, she had gone from a cute kid who seemed clueless about the value of a jar full of coins, to an ambitious future college student. Her attitude toward Will was hilariously responsible, like, "Sure, little brother—I'll do this fun project with you now, but I can't keep pooling my money with you forever. I've got plans and dreams of my own."

After reading this book, we wouldn't blame you for assuming that "saving for college" was an idea we'd planted in Anna's head. But we hadn't. We'd never even brought it up with her. Somehow—perhaps from eavesdropping on her older cousins—Anna had set a financial goal for herself, a *decade* away, and had determined it was her responsibility to make it happen.

It was only later after the kids were in bed and we were processing the moment, that we fully realized the weight of Anna's words. She had concluded that her money was meant for more than toys; that it was for long-term goals. She had concluded that it was her job, primarily, to make her dreams happen—not that her parents would pay for everything. And at eight years old, she had concluded that she needed to regularly put money aside, at the expense of short-term pleasures, to achieve her goals.

Over the course of writing this book, we've been implementing our own suggestions; we've initiated the conversations we recommend. The experience with Anna gave us a sense of hope and peace that, if something tragic were to happen to us today, we no longer have to worry so much about what might happen to our kids. Our lessons are in place, and our kids are starting to get it. There is room to grow and continue, but the baseline is there.

That's what every parent wants, isn't it? We want moments that indicate our children are starting to internalize the values we want to pass on. Time will tell if our kids ultimately take up the mantle of family stewardship, but we're hopeful that we're off to a good start.

We want to help our readers feel this same optimism and hope as they look to pass on their wealth, values, and financial smarts. In this book, we've given you a road map to undertake that process:

- **Create a Family Vision and establish an obligation to family stewardship.** Kids will absorb a set of values and perspective about what money should be used for, simply by interpreting the behaviors and attitudes you show them. You need to be *intentional* about making sure their takeaways are in line with your own vision for wealth, and raise them up to be family stewards by reminding them of their obligation toward future generations and society.
- **Show** your children healthy financial habits, like a strong work ethic, saving, enjoying, and giving. **Share** stories of your family history to help your kids understand the hard work that went into building the family wealth, discussing both the good and hard times. **Surround** your kids with positive financial influences, and protect them against negative influences by building up their financial literacy and introducing them to members of your financial team.

- **Teach your children financial literacy through providing them with financial experiences,** such as money management, budgeting, philanthropy, and investing. These experiences will be formulative, and will help your children become self-made, confident, financial leaders.
- **Build up other financial literacy fundamentals,** like learning the power of compound interest, the requirements of financial independence, and the difference between human capital versus financial capital.
- **Learn the important basics about investing, insurance, debt, and taxes,** so that your children understand how to use each area of finance strategically to *grow* their wealth. Failing to learn these basic concepts can easily lead to your wealth being *undermined.*
- **Effectively prepare your estate plan by organizing your information in a Personal Wealth Organizer, and maximize the efficiency of your wealth transfer by using relevant legal tools.** A well-organized and thoughtful estate plan is truly your last gift to your children, and the most direct way you can "pass it on." By using legal tools, you can maximize the efficiency of your wealth transfer, and protect your heirs from undue taxation.
- **Protect yourself and your heirs against bad financial decision-making by learning about dangerous biases, behaviors, and circumstances.** Much of the hard work you may have put into practice can be undermined if you or your heirs have unhealthy biases in place, or are negatively influenced by dangerous circumstances or untrustworthy people. Remember, if your goal is to pass it on, that your obligation is to future generations; seek to work on their behalf as you handle your estate.
- **Assemble a team** of trusted advisors to help you grow

your wealth, and to protect you and your family during tumultuous times. Appoint guardians if your children are still young and living at home. Appoint trustees to help guide your children when they are young, or as long into adulthood as you feel necessary.

When you implement these steps, you will have set your family up for success in passing on wealth, values, and financial smarts. However — that happy ending only arrives if you *apply* the knowledge and take action. Napoleon Hill, author of *Think and Grow Rich,* makes this point vividly:

> "Knowledge is only *potential* power. It becomes power only when, and if, it is organized into definite plans of action, and directed to a definite end."[43]

"Knowledge is power" is a falsehood. Knowledge is powerful only if you have a practical step-by-step approach to actually making something happen. You can know things — you can know everything — but if you don't have a plan for how to implement, be it transferring wealth to your children, creating financial literacy for your children, etc., the knowledge is just knowledge. We hope you now have the tools you need to translate your knowledge into powerful action.

In this book, we've included lots of little nuggets: Maintain a purpose for the family wealth. A value system must be taught to each generation. Make a contribution. Practice delayed gratification and "wait two weeks." Give money and talent as part of your wealth management strategy. Start

---

43 Hill, Napoleon, and Ross Cornwell. *Think and Grow Rich!* London: New Holland Publishers, 2019.

saving early. Invest in your human capital by making health and finance a life priority. Wealth management is a marathon. Be confident in your financial literacy so you're never led astray. Build a trusted team. Be thankful.

Still, all those bits of advice won't go any further than these pages unless you decide to take action for the sake of your children, and your children's children. Studies show that only 30 percent of people successfully manage to pass on their wealth beyond the third generation.

If you want to be part of the 30 percent that is able to successfully transfer wealth to your kids and grandkids and great-grandkids, and if you hope that they continue your wealth building into perpetuity—you have to set goals, then take action.

This is a worthy dream—and it's an achievable dream, provided you believe in it! If you assume that your endeavors will result in an automatic failure, then you won't get anywhere with passing it on. However, if you dream big and put these recommendations into action, you'll be able to give your future generations a leg up in this world.

What would that look like? Here's an idea.

In seventy more years, your grandchildren will gather together their own children and grandchildren at a family gathering. They'll tell stories of the sacrifices you made to build up the family wealth. They'll share tidbits of knowledge that you passed on to them, through stories and teachable moments. They'll review your family's vision, and the system of values that has been passed from generation to generation. They'll emphasize the importance of giving, and discuss new philanthropic ideas. There will be traditions of establishing financial literacy, and they'll be familiar with their team of financial experts. Your heirs will have built on your inheritance, pushing into new economic terrain as they pursue their own obligation to steward the family wealth.

We opened this book with a quote from Warren Buffett: "Someone is sitting in the shade today because someone planted a tree a long time ago." Let's be the one to plant that tree for our children. Let's teach them how to cultivate it, and nurture it. Let's look forward to the day when the tree has grown high, and bears fruit, and provides abundant shade beneath its wide-spreading branches.

Let's do that for our children, and for their children, and for their children's children. Let's pass it on.

APPENDIX

ASSEMBLING YOUR TEAM

"Teamwork is the ability to work together toward a common vision."

ANDREW CARNEGIE

Throughout this book, we've recommended that you seek out expert guidance for everything from drafting your estate plan, to diversifying your assets, to seeking out tax advice. Creating a team of experts who have your best interests in mind is also a crucial step to protect yourself against the dangers that can come in the midst of tragic circumstances.

In this appendix, we've created a straightforward reference guide to help you understand what to look for as you form your team. The key players on your team will look different, depending on where you or your children are at in their life stages. If your kids are still living at home, the most important two team members for you to identify are their trustee and guardian.

WHEN YOUR KIDS ARE UNDER 18: TRUSTEE AND GUARDIAN

If something were to happen to you while your children are still living in the home, you need to make sure they have good people to swoop in and care for them. The most important "team members" to consider when your children are still young are the **Trustee** and the **Guardian,** who may or may not be the same person.

If you have established a trust for your children then the **Trustee** will handle your children's money until they "come of age," whatever that age may be. A trust can be established to hold assets until any selected age and the trustee will be in charge of the funds under those terms. Some trustees work with "children" all the way until age 25, 35, or even an entire person's lifetime, depending on how the trust is designed. If and when your child wants to buy their first car, or an engagement ring, or a house, they'll need to request the money from the trustee in order to receive assets from the trust you created for them. The trustee may also be influential in determining major financial decisions, like approving a guardian's request to fund the child's private school education.

The trustee should be a person who you feel understands your values and goals for your kids. Sharing values and goals is important. Don't choose a trustee who has a completely dissimilar philosophy about money management than you, or they'll end up making financial decisions for your children that are wildly different than what you'd recommend. It is, above all, crucial that you trust your trustee. It should go without saying that you don't want to choose a trustee who would be tempted to steal or spend your money for their own benefit. You should have full confidence that the trustee will honor your wishes and work toward the best outcome for your children.

The trustee should also be knowledgeable and have the backbone to stand up to your kids, if need be. There's a good chance that one of your children might one day want to make a large purchase that would not be in their long-term best interest—say, an expensive car, or an over-the-top party. Perhaps an unsuitable trustee would let your kids have whatever they want, and not advocate for wiser long-term financial planning. A more appropriate trustee is someone who you can trust to look your kids in the eye and say, "This is not a wise investment, and I'm not going to let you have the money to do something that does not align with your parents' values and wishes."

If you are struggling to come up with family members that fit this role or are worried about the role causing conflict amongst family, you can select a corporate trustee. Utilizing a third-party corporate trustee can remove the emotion and potential family issues—they will have a process and formal approach to managing the assets and distributions. The downside of a corporate trustee is the added expense, along with less flexibility in decision making.

A child's **Guardian** is the person you select to raise your children. Your kids will live in their home, eat their food, and go to their church, fishing spots, rock concerts, etc. Once again, finding someone who shares your values is a critical consideration when selecting a guardian. The guardian of your children will pass on their morals, philosophies, and interests. They'll be in charge of nurturing and disciplining your children, influencing their pursuits, and guiding them in their goals. Choose someone that you trust and love—someone you know will love your children and raise them well.

The trustee and guardian are complementary roles, and many parents choose the same person to fulfill both responsibilities. That can be a good thing and a bad thing. In some ways, having the guardian also act as the trustee streamlines the financial component. If a child has to seek out someone other than their parent-figure every time they need money, that can get old quickly. As children grow up and require money for private school, eating out, or buying new school clothes, a guardian/trustee can spend the money set aside for that child, just as a parent might.

However, it also can become easy for a guardian/trustee to spend *through* that money quickly. Any number of expenses could be categorized as "in the child's best interest" of whatever standard the trust provides—trips abroad, new skis, a prom limo, and so on. It's also a risk that a trustee/guardian "skim off the top." Let's say that a college visitation tour for your child requires money for hotel rooms and gas, but rather than selecting affordable hotels to wisely steward the funds of the trust, the guardian/trustee decides they want to stay in a luxurious Hilton, which ends up unnecessarily wasting the funds they've been charged to maintain. Obviously, that's not what you'd hope for.

Having a separate trustee, on the other hand, ensures that there's a distinct line between "raising" the kids and providing for their financial future. Having different people serve the roles of guardian and trustee can more easily ensure you find "experts" in both categories—though, granted, it may produce some awkwardness when your brother realizes that you trust him to raise your kids, but not to handle their money.

The right decision is going to be different for every family. Also, consider that your nominated trustee and guardian may change over time. Your parents might be the obvious choice when they're 60 and your kids are four and six. However, what about when your parents are over 70, and your kids are getting into their turbulent teenage years? You may not feel like that would be the best option anymore. Revisit your nominations every few years, and make sure you still feel confident about your plan.

We recommend having several "back-up" options listed for each role as well. If you were to pass away suddenly, your first choice for a trustee and/or guardian may not be available. Maybe they moved to Australia, or the husband just lost his job and they're not in a strong financial position to take in multiple new family members. If you don't have several back-up options listed, the court will likely select your guardian for you. In such case, your children might be placed with their nearest living relative—whom you may or may not have wanted to be their guardian. Having three to four people listed for each role will ensure your kids are taken care of by people you trust.

SOURCING YOUR TEAM

Think back to Sam, whose parents died when he was in his young twenties; we discussed his story in chapter seven. For the first couple years following his parents' deaths, Sam wasn't sure where to turn. He was finally able to productively deal with his inheritance by getting plugged in with good advisors. Although Sam's situation worked out, we recommend getting a team in place *before* a crisis hits, so that you have plenty of time to establish trust.

A solid team of advisors would include three main experts: **a CPA, a financial advisor,** and **an estate planning attorney.**

Once you get one trusted team member in place, they can refer you to other people who would be a good fit for you, in the other roles. If someone like Sam comes to us, we'd help them assemble a team, because we work with plenty of CPAs and attorneys. The right attorney for Sam could be very different from the right attorney for a married, 50-year-old couple with two kids.

Part of our job is to scour the market to find the people who make sense for each individual situation. We interview people thoroughly. We understand their practices. We learn how the CPA will collaborate with the attorney and the financial advisor to help the client move forward as a whole.

You could hire one person to fulfill the role of a CPA, estate planning attorney and financial advisor. However, keep in mind that a single person probably won't have the full breadth of knowledge to apply to your situation. An individual who's building your portfolio and investing your money probably wouldn't also have time to write you a will or know the intricacies of the tax code. One person might brush the surface of each area, but they wouldn't get the necessary in-depth knowledge and strategy planning needed to do an excellent job.

Having a team in place like this can help protect you from being taken advantage of. In a collaborative team, people of different industries and companies watch over each other. Everyone is held accountable and works together. If you ask your financial advisor if they'd be willing to work with your CPA, their first response should be, "Absolutely." If they resist working with other professionals—that's a red flag.

When working to put a team together, we recommend that you start by asking for referrals from people you trust. Speak to friends and family members to find out what professionals they work with. Ideally, you should seek out referrals from people who seem to have made good financial decisions and may have similar financial complexities.

Alternately, you might want to seek out professionals who work with other people in your same line of business. Let's say you're selling a business, so you're likely going through a merger and acquisition firm that you've built a relationship with. Those people are experts in that space and have done the same thing for countless businesses of your size. Use those people as conduits to start assembling your team. Start by asking those experts for referrals.

In our opinion, referrals are a better way to go than internet searches. Some professionals which pop up on a Google search might have only been in the industry for two years, may not be credentialed, or may not be very skilled at their profession. With an internet search, you have no idea if you're finding trustworthy, honest, capable, or caring people. However, when you look through your professional network, you're more likely to find the right people for you.

Once you start meeting some of these advisors, ask each professional for their key accreditations, i.e., ask them if they're a CPA, CFP® professional, or CFA® charterholder. Have they shown commitment to their profession, and how? If you go to a company which only sells one product, you should recognize this as a *biased* business. Even if the product is something you need, you may not receive the most balanced recommendations from a person who is looking to sell you a product.

Let's talk about what to look for in each professional member of your team.

THE FINANCIAL ADVISOR

Your financial advisor helps you go on offense in *building* wealth, and will also help with protecting your wealth. A financial advisor helps you invest your money and build strategies for your long-term financial goals, ensuring your investments are aligned with your personal goals and objectives.

The financial advisor you choose will not only have access to intimate detailed information regarding your personal finances, but will also be the individual entrusted to manage your financial future. It's important that you feel trust for them! With that in mind, we recommend looking for these qualities:

- **Strong Ethics**: The integrity of your advisor is of the utmost importance. It is essential that you feel confident that your interests will always come first.
- **A Global Perspective**: In an ever-changing global econ-

omy, your advisor needs to have the resources and expertise to identify investment opportunities, both domestically and abroad.

- **Knowledge and Experience:** Managing your wealth is about much more than picking stocks or mutual funds; it requires an understanding of economics, corporate finance, asset valuation, and portfolio construction and management.

- **Commitment to Professional Development:** While there are a number of reputable credentials in the financial industry, CFA® charterholders and CFP® professionals take the greatest commitment and are widely respected. Part of maintaining these designations requires ongoing training in their field. They're also required to take a comprehensive evaluation of your entire range of financial needs and follow a strict code of ethics.

Find out about an advisor's communication process with their clients. Make sure they would be willing to collaborate with your CPA and attorney. Theoretically, anyone honest, ethical and straightforward should be able to answer all of your questions and back up their answers. They should be clear about their credentials, number of clients, assets under management, investment process, and communication process.

A holistic, CFP® professional will be more responsible for considering your entire financial picture. Personally, as financial advisors, we think about and manage the complete comprehensive picture from the broad purpose of our clients' lives. We help clients think through their five-, ten-, and twenty-year goals, concerns, bucket list items, and relationships, then we discuss how all those elements connect and intertwine. Our goal is to ensure that our clients' values and goals direct all the financial decisions and lead to the success of their families' current generation and beyond. In collaboration with tax specialists, estate planning attorneys, and insurance teams, we focus on how to help our clients achieve their goals and alleviate their concerns, whether those are related to health, children, or assets. The more we know about our clients, the broader our scope on their financial situations can be.

THE CERTIFIED PUBLIC ACCOUNTANT (CPA)

The tax code is enormously complex and constantly changing. Your family situation and wealth situation will also change over the span of your adult life. A trusted CPA will help you navigate all the complexities of the tax code as it meets your real life. They'll work with your financial advisor to identify opportunities for you, and help you manage your wealth strategically so that you don't end up paying more taxes than you're obligated to.

Once again, use your professional network to get referrals as to which CPA might be the right fit for you. Your financial advisor and attorney would be the ideal place to start because they will help you determine a good fit for your particular needs. Still, to determine which CPA is right for you, you need to ask yourself and the CPA several questions. For yourself, consider: Do you only need an annual tax return filed? Or do you have additional needs, like help with navigating the books for your small business? Do you need to file both individual and trust tax returns? For the CPA, you can interview them to find out the type of clients they serve, their communication process, and their tenure as a CPA.

THE ESTATE PLANNING ATTORNEY

The primary objective of an estate planning attorney is to ensure that your assets aren't unjustly taken and are efficiently transferred to family members or charities. They can also help you avoid the probate process or mitigate taxation.

Imagine Sara would like to give a third of her money to charity when she dies, but she can't give them her wealth just yet, since that's what she's living on. An attorney could help Sara create a charitable remainder trust, which she can use while she lives and which is given to charity upon her death; we discussed this in chapter six. Whether you have a charitable goal in mind or want to avoid/reduce estate taxes—your attorney can be your resource.

If privacy and confidentiality is a top priority, your attorney can help you align your estate in trust(s) so your estate distribution does not become public information at your death as a will would.

Many people think they don't need to start working with an estate planning attorney until they're old. In our experience, the estate planning piece should be done as soon as you start thinking about building your own wealth. Here are two examples that can illustrate why:

1. Anthony is a bachelor who inherited seven million dollars when his grandmother passed away. If he were to pass away suddenly with no estate plan in place, his

inheritance could get gobbled up by the cost of probate, be public record, and possibly incur estate taxes depending where the Federal Exemption Limit is at the time. If he'd put an estate plan together, many of these costs could have been avoided or minimized.

2. Allison and Brandon are a married couple with kids. They both work full time, and they each took out a life insurance policy. If they died suddenly, the children would receive sudden wealth through their life insurance claims. Ideally, the guardian and/or trustee put in place by the estate plan would take steps to manage and organize the wealth and raise the children.

Some people feel intimidated by the idea of seeking out an attorney, but it doesn't need to be that way. There are plenty of warm, approachable, casual attorneys who are prepared to offer both legal and emotional support to anyone going through the estate-planning process.

THE FAMILY OFFICE

Ultra-wealthy families (for instance, those with an estate valued at $100 million or more) often take the team-building to another level and form a Family Office. Essentially, they turn their family's wealth into its own business, creating a corporate infrastructure to manage all the family's various investments, assets, and philanthropic endeavors. They have a variety of experts and staff who manage their money so that their estate can grow and make an impact.

The team of expert advisors and investors which make up a Family Office can help your family expand and perpetuate your wealth for future generations. They'll help you and future generations maintain the vision for your family by offering the technical knowledge you might need to, for instance, maximize your charitable contributions, minimize estate taxes, and keep a hold on your family's long-term wealth goals.

Given that each person employed by a Family Office would receive his/her salary from out of the family's estate, this is a strategy used only by families with significant means. Although that might sound expensive, there's a reason wealthy families create these Family Offices: having expert guidance makes a big difference in what their estate ultimately produces!

THE VALUE OF A TEAM

By forming a trusted team of advisors, pursuing financial literacy within your family, and making sure that you communicate your vision and plans for your wealth, you are giving an invaluable gift to the people you love. You're able to mitigate the harm that could impact your family during dangerous circumstances and set them up for success in building financial literacy and growing their wealth.

ABOUT THE AUTHORS

ROGER AND LORI GERVAIS are proud parents of three wonderful children: Anna, Will, and Jack. Roger and Lori are also the husband-and-wife team behind The Gervais Group, named by Forbes as "Best in State Wealth Advisors" in Wisconsin. Lori, a CFP® professional, has been recognized for her commitment to clients and to the profession by Forbes, which named her to its America's Top Women Advisor List. Roger, a CFA® charterholder, uses his background in engineering to offer clients a unique set of problem-solving skills. Throughout their thirty years of combined experience in the industry, Roger and Lori have made it their mission to simplify the complex world of financial planning.

Made in the USA
Middletown, DE
24 October 2020